RAILWAYS IN AND A

MANCHESTER

The Changing Scene

Guide Bridge, early 1950s: The spire of St.Stephen's church on Guide Lane crowns this striking view of the eastern end of Guide Bridge station as B1 No.**61162** strikes away towards Woodhead and Sheffield with an Up express. The lines off to the right fanned out into an impressive array of sidings. This was Brookside Sidings located between the Manchester and Ashton-under-Lyne canal and the lines to Dukinfield and Stalybridge. Notice the lattice-post signal gantry; a pneumatically-operated array, this is a throwback from the same scheme as that mentioned at Ashburys. The end of steam on this route was almost nigh even in these far-off days. Catenary supports for the Manchester-Sheffield electrification programme are rising at the lineside and in a few years sights like this will be just a memory.
Tom Lewis

E. M. JOHNSON

ISBN 1 870119 36 3

Designed and Edited by Gregory K. Fox
Typeset by Bill Rear, Johnstown, Wrexham
Printed by the Amadeus Press, Huddersfield
Published by Foxline Publishing
32, Urwick Road, Romiley, Stockport. SK6 3JS

Foreword

Publications such as this have been described as part of the "Nostalgia Industry." Most of us occasion the odd delight, albeit sometimes self-consciously, in looking at pictures taken of ourselves, our family and our friends in times past. A well-known northern newspaper prints birthday congratulations juxtaposed alongside youthful-looking photographs of the celebrants. "Look who's 40 today!" or some such message, accompanies the picture. Something, perhaps, for the more brave, or reckless amongst us.

It was the legendary Faust who sold his soul to the Devil in return for the pleasures of unbridled youth-riches, power and love. Maybe, then, there is something of this ancient legend in all of us who want to look back in an attempt to recapture a moment of our youth, our past life, the area where we grew up, where our parents and grandparents lived, worked and, sadly, maybe died.

Looking today at the vast acreage of suburbia that surrounds cities like Manchester, Birmingham, Leeds and Liverpool, it is amongst the various modes of transport that, perhaps more than anything else, reflect some of society's biggest changes. As I walk down my local thoroughfare I am aware that, fifty years ago, most of the houses around me were in situ, altered little from the present day; the very same pavements rang to the feet of a previous generation. Overhead, though, the jet aircraft that scream and roar their way in and out of Manchester Airport would have sounded shocking to the eyes and ears my grandmother. As I write this manuscript the sounds of trains on the Manchester to Stockport and Styal lines can be heard clearly. What powers them today, though is not the LNWR and LMS Tanks, 4-6-0s, Pacifics and the like, but Class 86/87 and 90 Bo-Bo electrics, Class 158s, 304s, 305s, Sprinters; alien sights, to be sure, for any re-incarnated railway enthusiast.

Leafing through this book you may spot a once-familiar location, a lineside vantage point, the station you travelled from as a child, a bridge or thoroughfare you passed under or along in your schooldays. You may have licked ice-cream made in Godley, smoked Players' cigarettes, drunk Guinness like the Toucans or travelled to Morecambe on a day excursion. And if these were the riches of your youth, now, just like Faust, you can re-live those moments. I do hope you will enjoy them.

E.M. Johnson
Burnage, Manchester
August 1994

Brindle Heath Junction, April 13th.1962: "Austerity" 2-8-0 No.**90359** crosses the junction and tackles the stiff rising gradient (variously at 1-in-132, 1-in-88) on the Slow line with a train of wagon empties, probably for Agecroft colliery. This view paints a good picture of the complex layout in this area. Brindle Heath Junction signalbox-a 100 lever affair- sits in a fork between the Slow line and the Connecting line. Striding over the top of the empty wagon train are the massive girders of the flyover carrying the Fast line from Pendleton (Broad Street) towards Pendlebury. The mechanical coaling plant for Agecroft shed stands off to the right (Up side) of the Slow line; beyond this, part of the vast bulk of Agecroft Power Station juts out against the skyline. Just discernible, between the Slow line and the Connecting line, is Agecroft shed, its black engines sending forth plumes of steam into the bright Spring sky. *W.D.Cooper*

Introduction

Setting out with a camera in and around the Greater Manchester area to record something of today's railway scene has proved to be a most fascinating experience. What surprised me was the interest taken by casual observers in what I was doing. It seems the presence of a briefcase, an A4 ring binder, a clutch of pictures and a camera give one an official air, coupled with a degree of mystique. During my travels I have been mistaken for a planning official, a newspaper reporter, a lorry driver-and asked, yes, was I a "train spotter"?!

It is a changed world indeed that confronts the camera lens of the enthusuast in this, the last decade of the 20th century. I began my railway observations at the tender age of about four in the years immediately after the Second War. Wandering through the coal sidings at Mauldeth Road station on a Sunday morning with my father, a small boy gazed upon a railway little altered from that of his grandmother-a grand old lady who had watched trains on the Great Northern main line at Hadley Woods in the 1870s. My very youthful observations, contrasted with what I see today, provide a microcosm of the changes thrust variously upon our rail network over the last forty to fifty years.

Today's youngster visiting the same site would be accompanying his father on a trip, almost certainly by car, to the B&Q superstore, many former goods yards having been sold off by the railways for a broad spectrum of commercial uses. Passing along the railway can be seen a variety of passenger traffic: much of this is bound for Manchester Airport and, irrespective of starting point or destination, almost all of it is multiple-unit stock. What freight traffic exists consists of what we now call "Freightliners" en route, typically, for places such as Felixstowe and Southampton.

But the Introduction to a book should serve to whet the appetite of the reader: with that much, hopefully, done-we can pass along and begin our journey. First, though, some words of thanks.

Greg Fox has supplied his advice freely, both as a professional railwayman and a publisher. Ronnie Gee has, likewise, added his much valued assistance as a former signalman. My good friend Ray Hepner has again provided maps and prints from his collection which has greatly facilitated tracking down location details. I must make special mention of thanking Mr.W.D. Cooper for his tireless efforts in producing a superb selection of prints from the west side of Manchester and for the magnificent colour slide for our front cover. Grateful thanks are due, too,to Brian Green who has answered a never-ending series of requests for timetable and information on train workings. Valuable help with pictures has come from a wide variety of good friends all of whom I am indebted to.

Alex Appleton
Roderick Blencowe
Allan Brown
Alan Bryant
Gordon Coltas
John Clarke
(*Courtesy G.M.M.S.I.*)
Doug Darby
Jim Davenport
John Fairclough
Alan Gilbert
Brian Green
Timothy Grimshaw
David Ibbotson
Raymond Keeley
Bill Lees
Tom Lewis
Michael Mensing
Trevor Mosley
N. R. M.
Bill Potter
G.H.Platt
Keith Rathbone
Martin Shoults
Rachel Smith
Fred Walton

Dedication - I would like to dedicate this book to my Grandmother, Emily Compton. Granny's tales of seeing trains at Hadley Woods in her youth captured the imagination of a seven-year old boy. At the same age, the generous purchase for "Teddy" of a Hornby 0 Gauge clockwork train set helped to foster a lifetime's interest.

Parr's Wood Lane, border of Didsbury and Heaton Mersey Summer 1921: Many parts of South Manchester were still farmland in the period immediately after the First World War. Here, in those far-off days is a lovely scene: a rebuilt Midland Railway 4-4-0 No.**503** runs briskly down the 1-in-100/1-in-160 gradient from Heaton Mersey towards Didsbury on the last leg of its journey into Manchester Central. The train of seven coaches, most of them clerestories, has just cleared the overbridge at the junction of Parr's Wood Lane, Burnage Lane and Didsbury Road. Neat five-post fencing, in typical Midland style, marks off the company's boundary and a tidy shoulder of ballast fringes the permanent way. The trees are in leaf, wild flowers bloom, all appears well in the world and, no doubt, the driver, fireman and guard on board this train thought they part of an empire that would last for ever. No.503 was one of a number of Midland engines converted to oil firing to cope with the coal strike of 1921. Originally numbered 2421, 503 was one of 20 engines built as part of S.W.Johnson's supremely elegant "150" Class 7'-0" 4-4-0s by Sharp Stewart in 1899. *Collection of E.M.Johnson*

Flyover at Brindle Heath, looking towards Pendleton (Broad Street), August 12th.1960: Stanier 2-6-4 tank No.**42547** approaches the flyover on the Down Slow line and is signalled to take the connecting line down to Agecroft Junction with a 3-coach stopping train for Bolton via Clifton Junction. Immediately in front of the flyover abutment is the Goods line referred to previously: the lines off to the right were sidings and goods loops accessed from the Slow line and controlled by Irlam signalbox.
W.D.Cooper

Brindle Heath

Today's traveller from Manchester or beyond en route to, perhaps, Wigan, Blackpool or Southport will pay scant attention to the trees and shrubbery encountered as the train gathers speed and leaves behind the rather jaded westerly suburbs of Manchester and Salford. Thirty or forty years ago there were few such ramblings of nature to catch the eye, for instead of shrubs and wild greenery the eye would have focussed on a plethora of industrial trappings: cooling towers and power station chimneys, colliery winding gear, cotton mills, dye works and reservoirs. Around all this spider's web of industry there criss-crossed and burrowed a veritable web of railway lines-all controlled via a forest of semaphore signals.

Threading out north-westwards from Manchester Victoria were two main routes, both belonging to the former Lancashire & Yorkshire Railway: the Manchester and Bolton line via Clifton Junction dating from 1838 and the Pendleton and Hindley line of 1889. This railway-a four track system-began at Windsor Bridge Junction-actually controlled by Windsor Bridge No.3 signal box-and continued north-westwards via Pendleton (Broad Street). 900 yards beyond the latter, at Irlam signal box, the Fast and Slow lines parted company: a flyover at Brindle Heath Junction took the Fast line over the Slow line; at this point the Slow line spawned a "connecting line" which ran down a 1-in-69 gradient to reach Agecroft Junction. Here, the original line to Bolton, which had split at Windsor Bridge, was joined. At Agecroft Junction, also, a connection was provided for the lines in and out of Agecroft colliery.

On the east side of the connecting line-sometimes referred to as "The Agecroft Fork"-was the complex known as Brindle Heath sidings. Over to the west side was sited Agecroft engine shed-coded latterly 26B and 9J-and beyond this, the Agecroft colliery. The Fast and Slow lines came together again at Pendlebury where the Slow line bifurcated around an island platform. The P&H line continued on towards Hindley, via Swinton, Walkden (High Level), Atherton, Dobbs Brow and Crow Nest junctions to Wigan Wallgate.

Alongside the Bolton line, was to be seen the gargantuan outlines of Agecroft Power Station. Sited between the railway and the River Irwell, the cooling towers of this complex provide an unmistakable focus in our pictures of this area.

The three views on this and the adjoing pages show something of the sheer complexity of the track layout around Brindle Heath and Agecroft. Added to the traffic over the through lines was that generated by Agecroft engine shed, Agecroft Colliery, the one-time Agecroft Hall paper works and a power station bearing the same name. A veritable power house of industrial activity in the heartland of Lancashire.

Brindle Heath Junction, April 13th.1962: The camera has shifted a little to the right to reveal slightly different aspects of this incredibly fascinating place: "Crab" 2-6-0 No.**42724** blasts its way out of Brindle Heath Up sidings and on to the Up Goods line with a mixed freight train. The goods line continued to Irlam signal box, just under ½ a mile away, where it joined the Slow line. Interchange with the Fast line was provided at Pendleton (Broad Street). The four massive cooling towers in the background provide positive identification of nearby Agecroft Power station. *W.D.Cooper*

Site of Brindle Heath Junction, July 26th.1994: "The decline and fall of Industrial Lancashire" is the phrase I think best describes this view. Pretty well all of the industries mentioned in the previous captions have disappeared. As the district of Agecroft simmers on a sultry summer day in the last decade of the twentieth century, we can reflect for a moment on the area's demise. Agecroft Colliery and power station closed, the freight yard and adjacent sidings all gone, the motive power depot that supplied the prime movers for all the traffic now long redundant. Agecroft shed had closed on October 22nd.1966 and Brindle Heath signalbox closed on May 10th.1987. Walking the adjacent wasteland today, one finds a few bits of rail and scattered ballast lying interspersed with the odd rail chair and bits of point rodding. Perhaps the proponents of tree preservation could pay a visit to some of these sites: this is one commodity, at least, that is not in short supply. The former Pendleton & Hindley and Bolton lines still co-exist here, but the day and age of sophisticated junctions, a four-track layout coupled with a flyover are long past-something dictated by today's far less complex traffic patterns; the Fast lines had been taken out of use on November 21st.1965, Irlam box closed on December 19th.1967, Pendleton (Broad Street) on May 26th.1968. With the flyover gone and the connecting line removed, trains on the P&H line to Wigan and beyond take the route of the former Up and Down Slow lines. Amidst this barren landscape a two-car "Pacer" DMU forming a morning service from Wigan Wallgate to Rochdale via Manchester Victoria slows past the stunted remains of the flyover abutment. In the centre background can be seen the half-demolished remains of part of Agecroft Power station. *E.M.Johnson*

Agecroft Junction, July 1950: The area around Agecroft was beset with subsidence owing to the intensive nature of colliery workings in that district. The effects of such subsidence shows clearly in this official view of the former Lancashire & Yorkshire Railway signalbox. Situated on the Manchester-bound (Up) side of the line, the box was in dire straits showing a list towards the track at base-level of 9" when this picture was taken. *British Railways*

Agecroft Junction, looking to Brindle Heath, July 1950: An excellent view showing the track layout at Agecroft Junction. The connecting line along to Brindle Heath Junction, known locally as "The Crack", veers off to the right, the line from Bolton, via Clifton Junction, comes in alongside the front of the old signalbox. In the background, Park House Bridge Road crosses both sets of tracks. *British Railways*

Agecroft Junction, July 1950: Whatever the sentimental attractions for the traditional wooden-built signal box, it has to be said that time must march on and things must change. Though this, the replacement for the L&Y box, is by no means such an attractive building as its predecessor, the provision of an illuminated layout diagram, central heating and a built-in toilet must have been a welcome change for the signalmen that worked it. The replacement frame, sited at the back of the box, housed 57 levers and was to the (then) LMR standard design based on former LMS post-1943 practice. This itself was a modification of the former Midland Railway tappet frame. One spare lever, numbered 28, was provided. The brick-built box was sited on the Down side of the line, directly opposite the L&Y structure. Agecroft Junction signalbox closed on the weekend of April 9th & 10th 1988, the signalling from Windsor Bridge North Junction being taken over by stage 2 of the Manchester London Road power box extension. *British Railways*

Between Agecroft Junction and Brindle Heath, July 9th.1960: Standard Class 4 4-6-0 No.**75045** belonging to 27A (Bank Hall) shed runs along the Bolton line up from Agecroft Junction with a 5-coach stopping train bound for Manchester. The now-familiar outlines of Agecroft Power station's cooling towers stand out against the fleecy summer sky. Calling at Pendleton (Old) and then Salford, journey's end will be Manchester Victoria. The line in the foreground was termed the "Down Through Siding" and was under the control of Agecroft Junction box. *W.D.Cooper*

Agecroft, July 26th.1994: The rails are all-welded now and Class **150134** hums along with a late morning service into Manchester Victoria. An RMT signalmens' strike was due to begin at mid-day that day and this will be the last train for 24 hours. The former Through Siding now serves the Greater Manchester Waste Disposal Authority Terminal at nearby Cobden Street.
E.M.Johnson

Ashburys West Junction April 14th.1951: The skyline here was dominated by a magnificent lattice steel signal gantry; comprising pneumatically-controlled lower-quadrant semaphores, this dated from the widening and re-signalling of the line carried out by the Great Central under their dynamic young signal engineer, A.F.Bound, between 1904 and 1907. Branching off to the right is the line to Ancoats Goods and Midland Junction; from here a connection ran northwards to Philips Park and the former L&Y Ashton Branch to and from Manchester Victoria. Class J11, otherwise "Pom-Pom" No.**64435**, runs across the junction and into the station with the 11.35 am (SO) Manchester London Road to Marple. Rolling stock from the European rail network fills the sidings in the background. The Channel Tunnel was still some 43 years away. *J.D.Darby*

Ashburys

Ashbury's for Belle Vue: This station had the distinction, if not the peculiarity, of being named, not after a district, but a person. Put more correctly, one might say a factory, for in the immediate neighbourhood here was James Ashbury's carriage and wagon works, once one of the U.K's leading suppliers of railway rolling stock. Ashbury's was the second station out of London Road on the former Great Central main line from Manchester to Sheffield. The station was situated in the Openshaw district behind the junction of Ashton Old Road, a west-east thoroughfare (A635) connecting Manchester with Ashton-under-Lyne, and Pottery Lane. Ashbury's carriage and wagon works aside, here was an area world-renowned for locomotive excellence. Within a stone's throw of the station was the Armstrong, Whitworth works, the Otto Gas engine works (later Crossley Brothers), the Belle Vue locomotive shed of the former Midland Railway: just up the road was Gorton "Tank", home of the famous G.C.R. locomotive works, across from which was The Gorton Foundry, housing another locomotive builder-Messrs. Beyer, Peacock & Co. Ashbury's station was opened by the MS&L in 1855. It appeared as "Ashbury's for Openshaw" in Bradshaw's Guide for November of that year and "Ashbury's for Belle Vue" in the same guide for the following August.

Ashburys for Belle Vue, June 3rd.1954: The fine signal gantry has gone and steam is having its last fling on the Woodhead (Manchester-Sheffield) line as B1 No.**61127** gets into its stride with an express for Marylebone. The amount of rail-borne traffic in Britain in those days had to be experienced to be believed. Four tracks ran through here and the goods yards round and about would have been teeming with traffic when this picture was taken, witness the train of SNCF covered vans on the Slow lines beyond the Up platform. It is worth mentioning too, that no less than three routes to London were available to the 1950s rail traveller: via Sheffield to Marylebone, as seen here, via Derby to St.Pancras and the surviving route, the LNWR's line via the Potteries or Crewe to Euston. *B.K.B.Green*

Ashburys, March 30th.1994: A much-simplified traffic pattern exists through today's Ashburys. The Goods (Slow) lines are largely out of use and a rather depressing landscape of waste ground gives the traveller a vista of high-rise buildings looking over towards Beswick, Ancoats and Miles Platting. Class 305 **504** runs through the station forming a morning train to Glossop. Behind the EMU, still surviving, is Ashburys West Junction and the line northwards towards Philips Park. *E.M.Johnson*

Ashburys, March 29th.1994: The station is still alive and well, though now unstaffed. On the right a void in the brickwork shows where the platform waiting rooms once stood and at the far end of the opposite (Up) platform a solitary colour-light and "feather" protects Ashburys East Junction, a poor replacement for the magnificent multi-faceted semaphores of yesteryear. Notice the Up platform has gained a covered shelter, although it was unable to stop anything but the most vertical of rain showers. In September 1994, progress in the form of the Inner ring road, resulted in demolition of both the 1850's station building and the 1950's shelter. *E.M.Johnson*

Ardwick, Bennett Street Underbridge, March 21st.1957: One of a series of official photographs taken of structures prior to the onset of the Manchester-Crewe Electrification programme. One would hardly know, but the first day of Spring has dawned in Ardwick-a district of south-east Manchester. Off to our left is Manchester Corporation's Hyde Road bus depot (known locally as "Car Works"). The presence of the overhead wires (550v dc) shows this exit is used by Trolleybuses (service numbers 210-219). Under the bridge and over to the right can be seen some of Ardwick's long-gone streets: Rostron Street, Randolph Street and Ashover Street. Opposite these streets, and out of sight behind the railway, was the site of Manchester City's football ground before its removal to Maine Road in 1923. Notice the Morris Minor 1000 car and its companion, the Morris Traveller directly under the bridge; strange how yesterday's commonplace becomes today's treasure! In the background stands a building known as "Heywood House" an early example (note the chimneys) of the "high rise" type of development that was inflicted upon areas like Ardwick after the War. Elsewhere, little snippets of social history can be discerned: a schoolboy in the distance sports a plaid jacket, typical apparel for the youth of the later 1950s. Trilby hats and long raincoats are worn by the two men on the left; striding towards the camera is a figure sporting a flat peaked cap-almost certainly one of the corporation's bus crew going on duty at Hyde Road depot. Notice the lace curtains at all the windows of the terraced house by the bridge: no self-respecting housewife would be without such appendages in those days; privacy still ruled! Charles Atkinson & Co., toolmakers and precision engineers advertise their services on the bridge parapet. The original picture reveals the message: "vacancies for universal millers, tool room turners, tool-makers, universal grinder." In the left-hand corner reads a sign, placed almost as an afterthought: "girl age 15 to 17." Though we may never know what Charles Atkinson & Co. required of this young lady, there was ample employment locally in those days-even with the school-leaving age still set at 15. *British Railways*

Bennett Street, March 29th.1994: The deep parapets of the earlier bridge have been replaced by a simple-looking brick version, trolleybuses are long gone from the Manchester scene and the Ford Sierra has replaced the Morris Minor Saloon. Electric traction in this vicinity consists now of the 25 kv ac stock gliding effortlessly over the Manchester to Crewe line in and out of Piccadilly Station. Heywood House has disappeared and Rostron Close stands in place of Rostron Street, the two-up, two-down terraced houses supplanted by anonymous-looking maisonettes built, no doubt, to a standard Corporation specification. Charles Atkinson no longer require Universal Millers-swept out of existence like so many small engineering concerns. *E.M.Johnson*

Bolton, Trinity Street, 1950s: Bolton's Trinity Street station was a rather grand place. Opened in February 1904 the station replaced a previous two-platformed affair which dated from 1840. Trinity Street comprised two island platforms, each 1,116 ft.long. Pulling in alongside platform 2 with a lengthy express-almost certainly a Glasgow to Manchester train-is un-named "Patriot" 4-6-0 No.**45550**. The penultimate engine of a class which eventually totalled 52: this locomotive had been built in 1933 to a design of Sir Henry Fowler: a class sometimes referred to as "Baby Scots." No.45550 is coupled to one of the hybrid straight-sided tenders of 3,500 gallon capacity. Ten of these were built for "Jubilee" 4-6-0s, but some later found themselves coupled to other designs including ex-LMS 4Fs and 8Fs. The clock tower reads 4.55: sadly, this and all the station structure spanning the railway at street-level was to disappear in the rebuilding programme of 1987. The "Trinity Street" suffix was later dropped after the final closure to passengers of the town's other station-at Great Moor Street-in 1959. *N.E. Stead.*

Bolton

Bolton Station, July 21st.1994: A vast station with an immensely expensive fabric to maintain was not suitable for Bolton's modern-day needs. The passing of any item of railway history is a matter for regret; having said that, the railways have to live within a budget-often far from adequate-and a service of trains has to be provided. In consequence, we look on a Bolton much-changed since the days when lengthy, steam-powered Anglo-Scottish trains were daily callers here. In yellow, black and white Merseyrail livery, **150207** pays a morning call with a stopping service from Merseyside to Buxton. Along with Pacers and 158 Diesel multiple units plying their trade to Wigan, Southport and Kirkby, this is the typical Bolton scene nowadays.
E.M.Johnson

Bolton Station, August 11th.1975: Bolton is still a major freight and parcels handler in this view of almost twenty years ago. The impressive goods warehouse in the background was opened in 1904, parallel with the completion of the new passenger station. The spacious platforms are a reminder of the business once done here: the abundance of Wakes (cotton town annual holidays) excursions, through express departures to Scotland, Liverpool and North Wales as well as local traffic to towns in North Lancashire-Bury, Heywood, Castleton and Radcliffe-the latter now all gone. *British Railways*

Bolton Station, July 21st.1994: The long platforms remain, the roof retains its majestic sweep, but the track layout is simplified, goods facilities were withdrawn long ago and the rather splendid warehouse has been demolished. But..the platform buildings remain and are worthy of a visit. It is a shame that the tasteless "Docklands-Style" extension was visited on the buffet. Nevertheless, this offers quite good facilities and these are not on offer everywhere. *E.M.Johnson*

Bolton Station, August 11th.1975: Looking north-west to the end of the station and showing the splendid architecture of the buildings along Trinity Street to fine advantage. This end was the site of a triangle of lines and was known as Bolton West Junction: left to Lostock Junction and on to Wigan, Liverpool, Southport or Preston. Right to Blackburn, Burnley, Colne and all points in North and East Lancashire. Bolton West Junction can be seen in the background at the end of the right-hand platform. The top of the triangle comprised an avoiding line to the station for trains travelling from west (from the Preston direction) to east (towards Blackburn) and vice-versa. Known variously as the Johnson Street Fork, Bolton Avoiding Line (or Bolton Loop), it was taken out of use in January 1970. An unidentified Class 40 Diesel simmers on the Up Through line-that on the Down side has already been removed. *British Railways*

Bolton

Bolton Station, July 21st.1994: Something of an empty chasm is revealed following the removal of the Trinity Street buildings. Re-signalling has taken place and now "MP"-Manchester Piccadilly rules over all. The Up Through line has been done away with and the Class 40s are no longer operational. Multiple Unit stock now so typical over the whole rail system is none the less so here. A 2-car "Sprinter " unit prepares to move away from platform 4 forming a mid-morning service to Southport. *E.M.Johnson*

Bury, Bolton Street Station, November 8th.1950: A thoroughly wet and quite depressing scene at the Lancashire market town's Bolton Street Station. The dilapidated state of the roof suggests the reason for the photograph: this was one of a series of official views taken by the Civil Engineer's department prior to the commencement of rebuilding work. The reconstruction was concentrated mainly at street-level and comprised the rebuilding of the station frontage, booking hall and footbridge. The gentleman sheltering from the rain appears to be looking at an advertisement for "Zal" disinfectant: items on offer on the W.H.Smith bookstall include The Christian Science Monitor, Radio times-"again on sale", and Picture Post-"ready to wear fashions in colour." For the adventurous townspeople of Bury, the Competitor's Journal offered "tons of money to be won weekly." Anyone wishing to get away from the rain and have a breath of sea air could take an evening excursion to Blackpool the following Saturday: departure from Bury was at 4.58, returning from Blackpool (Central) at 11.00- and all for the princely sum of 4/6d (22½p). *British Railways*

Bury, Bolton Street, July 31st. 1994: The rebuilt station frontage was completed in the summer of 1952. Though fairly plain and austere-looking, some considerable thought appears to have gone into providing up-dated facilities. New entrance doors "of polished Nigerian walnut" and "entrance and columns faced with Terrazzo" are two examples from contemporary literature. The London Midland Region Architect Mr.J.M.Harrison under the direction of Civil Engineer Mr.J.Taylor Thompson were responsible for the design work. Today, to the unitiated, Bolton Street may appear to be a working BR station-a view taken in the late 'fifties maybe. Bolton Street Station is, of course, a working station, but is now the home of the East Lancashire Railway (ELR)-a thrusting and well-organised preservation movement who have made their base here since BR closed the station in March 1980. Since then, BR moved Manchester-Bury electric services to a new Interchange Station with the local bus network: this is sited just a few minutes walk away, nearer to the main shopping centre. Though BR passenger services from here to Ramsbottom were lost (in 1966) and to Rawtenstall (in 1972) they have since been re-instated thanks to the very creditable efforts of the volunteers of the East Lancashire Railway. At the time of writing, the line eastwards to Heywood has been accessed and regular steam services to the town are planned from mid-1996. This will give the ELR a link with the former BR network and offers yet more exciting possibilities. *G.K.Fox*

Bury, Bolton Street, October 26th.1950: Bolton Street Station was a five-platform affair with both terminal and through facilities. Manchester-Bury services terminated here, though at one time reached the northerly village of Holcombe Brook via Tottington Junction on the Accrington and Bacup lines. Originally electrified, the severely graded route to Holcombe Brook had reverted to steam working for twelve months, before closure in 1952. This is a view looking north towards Ramsbottom and Rawtenstall; notice the wooden shrouding for the side-contact conductor rails. At 1200v Dc this was something of a hybrid system, being double the voltage used by the L&Y on its Merseyside system. Though the 1951-52 rebuilding programme at Bolton Street left the platform structures largely untouched, the magnificent three-storey building on the right, the headquarters of the (old) East Lancashire Railway Company, was demolished later on. *British Railways*

EAST LANCASHIRE
LIGHT RAILWAY CO. LTD.
PLATFORM TICKET
VALID DATE OF ISSUE ONLY
Issued subject to Company Conditions
10 | 11 | 12 | 1 | 2 | 3 | 4 | 5
Hackings (Printers) Church
6778
P5

Bury, Bolton Street, July 31st.1994: The lengthy canopies have gone from platform 3 and the absence of fine old headquarters building now gives an uncluttered view of the Bury skyline. The traditional maroon enamelled sign gives a clear indication as to the function of the surviving platform building! *G.K.Fox*

Bury, Bolton Street, looking towards Manchester, October 26th.1950: Station architecture seems a sorely neglected topic; this fine view of the former East Lancashire Railway headquarters shows something of the abundant confidence and style endowed by the Victorian railway pioneers. Demolition took place in the 1970s. depriving this side of the station, at least, of something of its former glory. *British Railways*

Bury, Bolton Street, July 31st.1994: Bolton Street Station must hold something of a unique position in railway preservation. Where else, one wonders, has steam re-appeared in a railway environment where electric services previously dominated? The conductor rails have gone and the buildings now echo to what is probably the best selection of preserved steam on offer anywhere. The building rising alongside the far platform is a new restaurant and cafe for the East Lancashire Railway. Though by no means as splendid as the previous East Lancs structure, it offers some interesting architectural details: the same cannot be said for the nondescript office block in the background. *G.K.Fox*

Radcliffe Central Station, looking to Bury, July 29th.1959: This Lancashire town, a close neighbour of nearby Bury, once had no less than four railway stations within what was a fairly small boundary. Radcliffe Central was later emasculated when the line westwards to Bradley Fold via Ainsworth Road closed in October 1970. This cut off access to Bolton (Trinity Street)-the line north-eastwards from Bolton to Bury's other station at Knowsley Street (via Radcliffe Black Lane) closed at the same time. Then newly-rebuilt, Radcliffe Central looks smart and pristine in this summer view. With the advent of the Metrolink takeover of the Bury line, from April 6th.1992, a large car park was provided at Radcliffe: a thoughtful opportunity that could have been usefully provided at other locations. To the left and out of the picture, the spur which connected the line from Bolton via Bradley Fold Junction with the line from here to Bury at Radcliffe North Junction. With Metrolink now looking at a number of other options for expansion, the loss of the 4¾ mile link from here to Bolton can only be regretted. *British Railways*

Radcliffe Station, July 31st.1994: The side-contact conductor rails have gone, along with the 1950s-style concrete lamp posts, the telegraph posts and semaphore signalling. Metrolink are now in charge and overhead electrification at 750v Dc now rules the day. Glassless buildings are a pre-requisite now-less damage through vandalism. The familiar green Metrolink logos, all part of the organisation's "house style", look at least as interesting as BR's collectable totems. LRV No.**1021** *The Greater Manchester Radio* departs with the now customary swiftness and quietness for Bury. *G.K.Fox*

Chinley, looking East, c.1960: A splendid view with not a train in sight! The station buildings, goods yard and Chinley Station North Junction signalbox stand out clearly against a backdrop of the Derbyshire hills. To the right, the goods yard is deserted and close scrutiny reveals no traffic present. The tracks on the left were designated Slow or "Sheffield" lines, those to the right Fast or "Manchester" lines. Continuing on to Chinley North Junction, just one mile further along, and the lines parted company: those on the left to Sheffield via the Dore and Chinley line, popularly known as the "Hope Valley" route, the tracks on the right curved away to Peak Forest, Ambergate, Derby and London St.Pancras. *D.Ibbotson*

Chinley. June 4th 1994. Totally reduced to a plain line operation, albeit either side of a still substantial island platform, Class 101 dmu heads towards Manchester along the formation formerly occupied by the "Up" line to London. Almost a century after the railway was quadrupled, it finds itself back to basics once again. *E.M. Johnson.*

Chinley

Chinley, looking East from Platform 6, 1950s: Most St.Pancras expresses called at Chinley and here one such train rolls in to the station. A fine Summer day sees "Jubilee" No.**45665** *Lord Rutherford of Nelson* at the head of a 9-coach working in the famous "blood and custard" livery of the 1950s. Once clear of Chinley, it was downhill, almost, all the way for the nineteen or so miles into Manchester Central with some high speed running guaranteed.
Author's Collection

Chorlton-cum-Hardy Station, September, 1960: "Britannia" Pacific No.**70032** *Tennyson* roars through the station with the 4.25 pm express from Manchester Central to St.Pancras. Coming onstream in the early Summer of 1958, these modern Pacifics were the first such types to regularly haul Midland line trains over this route. As a young enthusiast at this time I had been accustomed to the sight of Black 5s, "Jubilees" and the odd "Royal Scot" on the St.Pancras expresses: small wonder, then, that the first sight of a "Britannia" here caused such a stir! This had been an exciting year; crowned by the arrival of the "Midland Pullman" on July 4th.-a wonderful sight in its two-tone Nanking Blue livery and Pullman crest up front. Happy memories indeed.
W.A.Brown

Site of Chorlton Station, May 15th.1994: Chorlton Station had closed as far back as 1967 and, though the line-later singled-lingered on until 1988 for Freightliner traffic from Trafford Park, the site here had long assumed an air of dereliction following closure of the South District line to through traffic south of Chorlton Junction in May 1969.

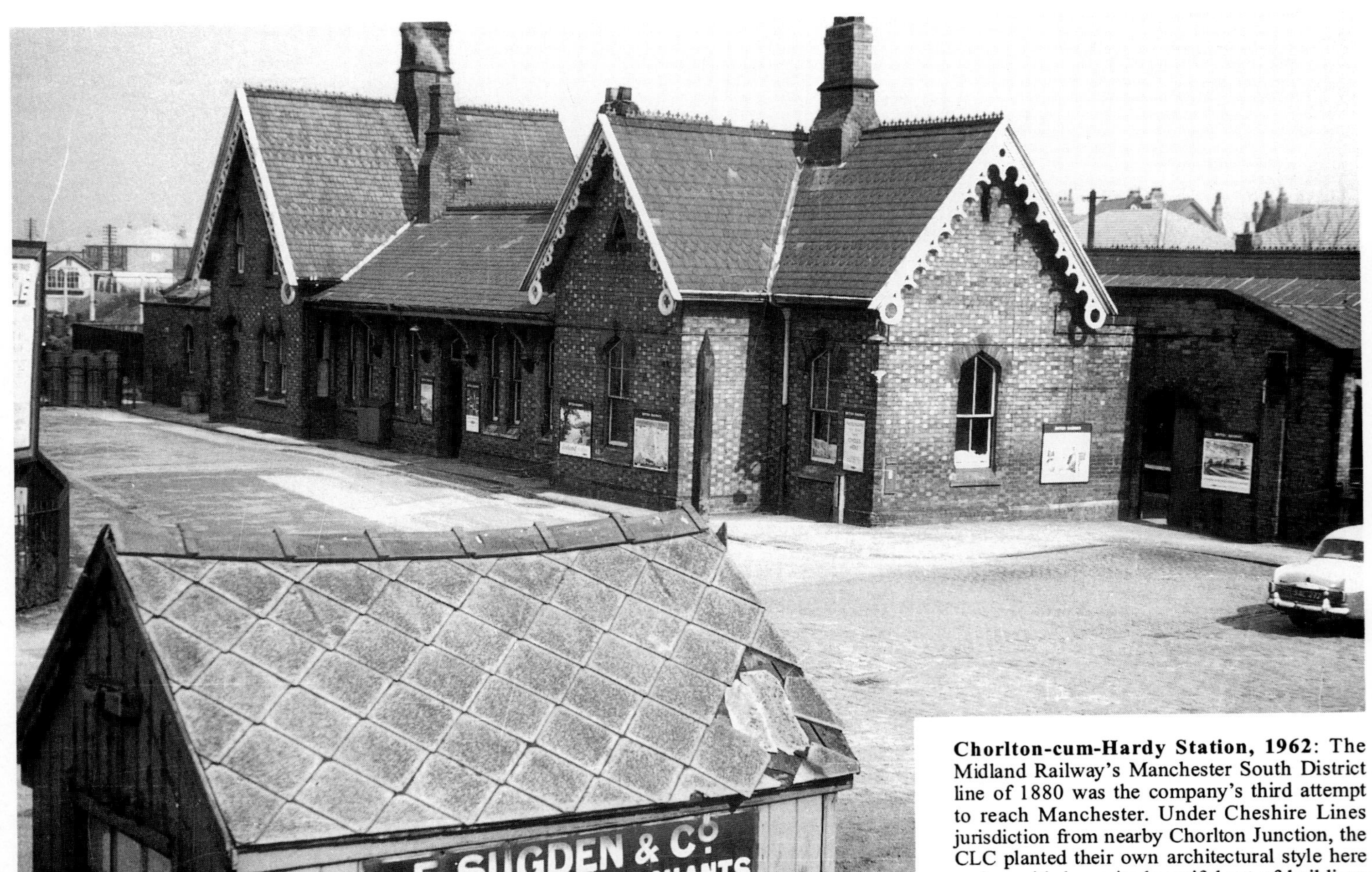

Chorlton-cum-Hardy Station, 1962: The Midland Railway's Manchester South District line of 1880 was the company's third attempt to reach Manchester. Under Cheshire Lines jurisdiction from nearby Chorlton Junction, the CLC planted their own architectural style here and provided a quite beautiful set of buildings into what was then a quite corner of South Manchester. Today, when so much station "architecture" consists of little more than bus-type shelters, we can only stand back in awe to admire the exquisitely inlaid brickwork, delicately-fretted bargeboards and patterned slates, topped by a cast iron ridge. Even E.Sugden's coal office has style to the roof! The station signalbox can be glimpsed through the gap to the left of the station buildings.
G.H.Platt

Chorlton-cum-Hardy, April 17th.1994: Today, a Safeway supermarket covers the station land and trains no longer pass this way now; the last to do so ran through on Saturday, October 15th.1988-the 15.54 Trafford Park to Southampton Freightliner diverted this way owing to re-modelling work on platforms 13 and 14 at Piccadilly. All, though, may not be lost here: under current Metrolink expansion plans-dubbed "Metrolink 2000"-the railway would be re-instated from a point in the vicinity of what is now Trafford Bar station. Re-gaining the old alignment south of the site of erstwhile Throstle Nest South Junction, Chorlton would be served by Metrolink en route to Manchester Airport. Ambitious plans which, it is to be hoped, come to fruition.
E.M.Johnson

Chorlton Junction, August, 1920: Less than a mile south of Chorlton-cum-Hardy station, at Chorlton Junction, the former Great Central line to Fairfield parted company with the Midland's route south via the Peak. Here, we step back into another world as a lady with a parasol watches J.G.Robinson's Class 1 4-6-0 No.**427** *City of London* cross the junction with the 3.22 p.m. express from Manchester Central to Cleethorpes. No.**427** is in the Great Central's black goods livery; lined red and white and adorned with brass beading and nameplates, these were splendid, powerful-looking locomotives, though their looks belied what was a somewhat mediocre performance. The 6-coach train is composed of teak-bodied clerestory stock-in sharp contrast to the Midland's distinctive crimson lake which would have been a regular sight here in those days. *G.M.Shoults*

Chorlton Junction

Site of Chorlton Junction, May 15th.1994: All signs of rail traffic have long vanished as we gaze on the sad and sorry sight that once was an important focus of South Manchester's railway system. Yet there is hope: under the current "Metrolink 2000" project there is an imaginative plan to extend Manchester's LRT system from a point near Trafford Bar (formerly Old Trafford) over to Manchester Airport. This would involve use of this section of the alignment as far as Mauldeth Road West, about half a mile south-east from here. One small step at least to reclaim something of this ballast-strewn wilderness. *E.M. Johnson.*

Bridge spanning Clare Road, Levenshulme, December 10th.1959: One of a series of official pictures taken in the late 1950s no doubt to record aspects of civil engineering to be undertaken in connection with the impending electrification of the Manchester to Crewe line. This railway was carried mostly overland between the two centres, throwing up in its passage some very impressive structures. Though by no means in the same league as the famous Stockport and Holmes Chapel viaducts, this rather humble edifice is nevertheless typical of many thousands of underbridges that make up part of what is nowadays termed "the railway infrastructure." A brick-built structure covering a minor road of no particular consequence, yet, strangely it is the very simplicity of such a structure that makes it, somehow, worthy of inclusion: how many of us railway modellers, for instance, could make an accurate model of such a simple-looking bridge? How many times have we passed beneath such an arch, never even giving it a first, let alone a second, glance? The whitened stone springers beneath the arch highlight the abutments, the distance between which, when approached by traffic from the Errwood Road side (behind the camera), is narrower than the actual roadway. The vehicle heading up towards the A6 (Stockport Road) is one of the once-familiar coal lorries which plied their trade in suburbia. Gladly, their days have gone, along with coal fires and the filthy, life-threatening, choking smogs. *British Railways*

Levenshulme

Clare Road, March 5th.1994: The air in Manchester is much clearer now! Little has changed in the intervening years: the curious-looking lamp posts, always painted green in Manchester, have given way to reinforced concrete specimens of a type now seen everywhere. The "overhead" now powers the trains that rattle and roar over this little part of suburbia, and the trees, soon to show their verdant cloak, seem more prolific. Life in Clare Road goes on. *E.M.Johnson*

Denton Junction

Denton Junction, September 7th.1960: The hey-day of the railways saw places of relatively minor importance themselves become centres of thriving activity. Such an area was Guide Bridge and Denton where lines of no less than seven different companies converged and interacted with one another in a plethora of traffic movement. At Denton , even in the early 1960s, one could still see an impressive junction, still with some pre-Grouping signalling, handling a type of traffic that had changed little from Victorian and Edwardian days. Three routes converged at Denton Junction: 8F No.**48682** is coming off the LNWR's Stockport to Guide Bridge line with a local freight from Cock Lane (Guide Bridge). To the right is the line through Hooley Hill Tunnel via Dukinfield and Ashton to Stalybridge closed to freight traffic on April 28th. 1968. Passenger traffic had ceased some years earlier, on September 25th.1950; though the line had been used for through passenger trains until January 1st.1968. LNWR-pattern signals still survive to protect the line on the left; this picked up connections from Ashton Moss, Crowthorne, Droylsden, Oldham, Manchester and Stalybridge which were fed towards Stockport.
Gordon Coltas

Denton Junction, March 29th.1994: The Stockport to Guide Bridge line has shrunk now to almost nothing; freight trains still run, but, at the time of writing, passenger traffic has been reduced to the level of one train per week: the 13.56 FO Stockport to Stalybridge which returns as empty coaching stock! The alignment off to the right-the Hooley Hill line-has been replaced by "The Hawthorns", a smart-looking residential development standing to the rear of Corporation Road. The residents will not be disturbed by the sound of trains; such is the meagre level of traffic nowadays. *E.M.Johnson*

Denton Junction, 1958: Mention has been made elsewhere of the decline of small engineering businesses in areas such as Manchester. This picture, taken from the rear of a train travelling from Guide Bridge to Stockport, shows another aspect of this fascinating junction. The LNWR signalbox, still extant, stands in front of the premises of the Planet Foundry Company, quite a sizeable concern who had their own private sidings here. The wagon empties, which has just clattered past, would be an unwelcome intrusion into the tranquility of "The Hawthorns" today. *G.H.Platt*

Disley Tunnel, n.d: The wild and beautiful Derbyshire countryside made a perfect backdrop for railway photography. One such exponent of this art was the late Alan Bryant who concentrated much of his work in the area around Disley and New Mills. Alan's camera has caught "Royal Scot" No.**46162** *Queen's Westminster Rifleman* heading south towards the Peak District with the Up "Palatine"-2.25 p.m. ex Manchester Central to St.Pancras. Lingering clouds of smoke and steam around the mouth of the 3866 yard tunnel await the crew of a loaded ICI Hopper train in the Down loop alongside the signalbox.
A.H.Bryant

Disley Tunnel, June 4th.1994: Viewed from the same lattice steel footbridge alongside Redhouse Lane, encroaching foliage has all but obscured the sight of Makin's paper mill which appeared in the background of the previous photograph. Though simple in outline, this picture is a substantial statement of the changes that have been wrought on the British railway system over the last two decades or so. Signalling systems have become centralised and the lineside signalbox, so long a characteristic of the wayside rail scene has vanished. Trackwork has become less complex: out of the necessity to reduce maintenance costs, and here, as elsewhere, goods loops-required to put slow-moving, loose-coupled freight trains "inside"-are with us no longer. The train in our picture, **158778** forming the 12.16 Manchester Piccadilly to Cleethorpes could be described as typically modern. Short, well-filled, some would say over-filled, Diesel units now ply cross-country routes on a regular interval basis. Gone, too, the wooden-sleepered track, replaced by long-welded rails sitting on heavily ballasted concrete sleepers. Such are the changes, should we lament them?
E.M.Johnson

Approach to Disley Tunnel, mid-1960s: Turning away from the tunnel mouth we look south-eastwards in the direction of New Mills and Chinley. Approaching on the descending 1-in-132 of the Down line, a gentle whisper of steam escaping from the safety valves, is Austerity 2-8-0 No.**90242** with a train load of coal, loose-fitted, bound, no doubt, for one of the Lancashire power stations. *A.H.Bryant*

Disley

Approach to Disley Tunnel, c.1985: The trains carrying limestone in bogie hopper wagons from Tunstead Quarry to the former ICI works at Northwich have had an amazing variety of motive power over the years. This is hardly surprising as the traffic has been carried in this type of wagon since 1936. From the early 1980s pairs of Class 20 Diesels were rostered on to "the Hoppers"; this gave observers the chance to view some of BR's oldest motive power hauling a clutch of almost vintage rolling stock! **20 305** is in tandem with an unidentified class mate passing the same spot as our Austerity 2-8-0. Gone now are the sidings and goods loop, the semaphore signal and attendant signal box. The beckoning hills follow the same outline, but notice the rapidly encroaching screen of trees alongside the Up line. Now the Class 20s have gone, "The Hoppers" still roll and the trees are bigger....... *A.H.Bryant*

Diggle Station, n.d: The driver of "Jubilee" No.**45647** *Sturdee* casts a backward glance at his train, the 09.15 SO Leeds to Llandudno as it emerges from Standedge Tunnel and races through Diggle station. Cross-Pennine traffic had necessitated the construction of two sets of tunnels at Standedge. The first had been driven through in 1849 and a second was completed in 1870. This remained the longest railway tunnel in Britain until the opening of the Severn Tunnel in 1886. To cope with ever-increasing volumes of trans-Pennine traffic a further, double-track bore, was opened in 1894. This last of the Standedge tunnels was most unusual in that it contained water troughs. These were sited just inside (this) the Diggle end. The troughs drained into the Huddersfield and Ashton canal which ran under the Pennines between the new and old tunnels. Diggle Station closed to passengers on September 9th.1964. "Sturdee" was withdrawn from service in April, 1967.
John Clarke courtesy The Museum of Science & Industry in Manchester

Diggle

Site of Diggle Station, March 29th.1994: Admirals are not commemorated on the sides of Class 142 railcar sets; only a painted number now identifies one Regional Railways "Pacer" set from another. This is unit **142 014** making up the 12.25 Wakefield Westgate to Manchester Victoria. The platforms of Diggle Station have been reduced to a grassy bank and the line speed limit has been raised to 60 miles per hour. Notice the pointing on the right-hand side of the tunnel portal appears to have weathered little in about thirty years; truly a healthy, clean environment! *E.M.Johnson*

Diggle Junction, c.1950s: The convergence of two separate routes, a local station, a goods yard and a separate wagon sidings fused together at Diggle to provide a most interesting and quite impressive small-scale rail centre. The Pennines, "the backbone of England" to schoolboy geographers, had been pierced by the tunnels of no less than four separate railway companies. Diggle Junction fronted onto one of these, the tunnels at Standedge-at 3 miles, 66 yards, terminating immediately behind Diggle station -barely perceptible at the back of the view. The junction proper was formed by two lines: on the left the main line to Huddersfield-dating from 1849 and to the right the line from Stalybridge via Micklehurst, essentailly a relief line-which had opened in 1886. The sidings on the left were for wagon empties-principally from coal traffic emanating from various Yorkshire pits. Some of these were collected from stations in the Oldham area, others came from the Friezland gas plant and the power station at Millbrook, near Stalybridge. In the background a plume of steam betrays an approaching train clearing the platforms of Diggle Station, a Local with a Black 5 in charge and six coaches behind the tender. *Author's Collection*

Diggle Junction, March 29th.1994: Today, the once-busy signalbox has been reduced in status to nothing more than a block post between Greenfield and Marsden-on the Yorkshire side of the tunnel. With the run-down in freight traffic and the attendant absence of slow-moving trains, there was little need for the Micklehurst line-closed in 1966. A swathe of fine trees screens the land where the wagon empties were once packed. Reasons are abundant: on the domestic front, the decline in the use of coal as a fuel, the loss of much heavy industry and the switch to other fuels-notably natural gas-has caused a deep erosion in the amount of coal traffic over and through the Pennines. An absence of the railway paraphenalia of yesteryear-semaphore signals, telegraph posts, watertank and goods shed paints a strikingly different canvas. And yet, the railway through Diggle today is busy enough: a steady stream of passenger traffic to and from Liverpool and Manchester providing the mainstream of activity here. *E.M.Johnson*

Droylsden Junction, November 4th.1929: Droylsden is famous as the home of Robertson's Jams. It offers nothing pretentious to the railway student and the environs hereabouts are not linked to events of any great moment. This official view was taken after an accident to a certain Mrs.Platts. Possibly, the LMS company's lawyers would have wanted some sight of the location-pending, maybe, a case for compensation. Whatever this unfortunate lady's fate, the picture shows well an island platform between two sets of rails, a tidy brick-based signalbox and some rather interesting details. This is territory belonging to the former Lancashire & Yorkshire Railway. The company's Ashton Branch, from Stalybridge into Manchester Victoria via Ashton Moss North Junction lies to the right. Branching off from this, over to the left of the island platform, is the former LNWR's line to Denton Junction-the Ashton Branch Junction Line-via Ashton Moss Junction. An LNWR sign cautioning against trespass and a distinctive oval bridge numberplate, numbered 16, form an interesting contrast to neighbouring L&Y sundries: the "switch" plate alongside the base of the signalbox warning of the protecting catch points, a superb "passengers must not cross the line...." and, of course, the omni-present, warning against trespass headed "PUBLIC NOTICE". Just beyond the junction Home signal can be discerned an LNW/L&Y boundary marker.
National Railway Museum

Droylsden, March 29th.1994: Few of the contrasting pictures presented in this work present more of a marked difference than this one. To the casual observer this is a totally different place: and indeed, in many respects, it is. Droylsden Station closed its doors to passengers on October 7th.1968, the line down to Ashton Moss Junction was taken out of use on 6th July 1969. After taking this picture, Greg Fox and myself picked our way over the site; as we did so we stumbled across some hefty chunks of the chequered setts that formed the platform surface and show themselves quite clearly; just about the only tangible remains, for almost all traces of a station here have vanished. Perhaps the ghost of Mrs.Platts can tell us what happened on that November day of over sixty years ago. *E.M.Johnson*

Droylsden Station, n.d: Droylsden in happier times is viewed here as Stanier Class 4MT 2-6-4 Tank No.**42551** calls with the 3.30 p.m. Manchester Victoria to Mossley train. The station buildings on the left straddle the island platform; the converging lines of the junction can be feintly discerned beyond the protruding canopies. *J.Davenport*

Eccles, May 6th.1957: "Jubilee" No.**45583** *Assam* pulls away from Eccles on the Up Slow line with a seven coach stopping train. The terraced houses, adjoining each other on the thoroughfare known as "The Park" were strongly characteristic of this part of industrial Lancashire. The three semaphore arms controlled respectively the crossovers from Slow to Fast lines, the entry to Stott Lane exchange sidings and the Ship Canal branch. *W.D.Cooper*

Eccles, June 2nd.1994: Eccles today, almost forty years on from the previous pictures, is a much-changed place. The Slow lines have been taken out of use and the M602 Motorway has long since swept away all the houses that stood along The Park together with the two churches as well. Just visible beneath the encroaching foliage are the remains of the old Up Slow line platform, the thick screen of vegetation acting as something of a barrier to the incessant noise from the motorway behind. The track on the right is the sparsely used neck of the line down to the Manchester Ship Canal. *E.M.Johnson*

Eccles

The railway between Manchester and Liverpool via Eccles, Earlestown and Rainhill is amongst the oldest and most historic in the world. This stretch of line, forever immortalised by Stephenson, the "Rocket", Huskisson and the Duke of Wellington was to quickly become a life-giving artery between Manchester, in Victorian times a teeming industrial slum, and Liverpool a thriving commercial port and once the gateway to what must have seemed like the entire universe. The line through Eccles was later quadrupled and a branch down to serve the Manchester Ship Canal was opened in 1895, the original L&M line having become part of the mighty London & North Western empire as far back as 1846.

The four-track section of the Manchester to Liverpool line continued westwards from Eccles to the suburb of Salford and small Lancashire township known as Patricroft. Those Mancunian enthusiasts with a bent towards number-taking, train spotting or shed bashing-call it what you like-will, doubtless, remember this location for its locomotive depot. Designated variously 10C, under Wigan-Springs Branch until April 19th.1958-and then 26F-as a sub-shed of Newton Heath, before becoming 9H under Longsight, Patricroft shed was sited in a triangle of land between the main line from Eccles, the line northwards via Clifton Junction to Bury and the line north-westwards from Eccles Junction via Monton Green and Worsley to Bolton.

Patricroft Station, October 1958: Approaching from the direction of Eccles and Manchester is Rebuilt "Patriot" No.**45531** *Sir Frederick Harrison* with the 11.45 am Leeds City to Llandudno (1.35 ex Manchester Exchange) train. Patricroft locomotive depot is clearly marked behind the signalbox; the concrete coaling plant was part of a modernisation programme instituted by the LMS in the mid-1930s. On the right is Hampden Grove; access to the shed was via the footbridge in the foreground. *W.D.Cooper*

Patricroft

Patricroft Station, June 2nd.1994: Patricroft was one of the last surviving steam depots around Manchester, managing to exist until June 29th.1968. Now, nature has returned to reclaim the land which stood for so long as one of the key rail heads in the Manchester area. On a dull Summer day "Sprinter" Unit **156441** pulls away towards Salford and Manchester with a stopping train from Liverpool. Hampden Grove is a quieter place now. *E.M.Johnson*

Patricroft Station, May 28th.1963: At the opposite (west) end of the station the four-track section continued over almost level ground to Barton Moss Junction where the line became restricted to a conventional two-track layout. BR Standard Class 5 No.**73048** enters the station with an express, probably from North Wales, on the Up Fast line in the direction of Manchester Exchange. *W.D.Cooper*

Patricroft Station, June 2nd.1994: Barton Moss Junction signalbox appears to be out of use and the formation here has long since dwindled to two tracks, such is the dramatic reduction in the amount of traffic over the last twenty-five years. "Pacer" Class **142036**, a type sometimes referred to rather ungraciously as "Bendy Buses"-runs in to Patricroft forming a stopping train from Liverpool Lime Street to Manchester Victoria.Overgrowth in the background, along with car-parking spaces, has long since covered the path of the former Slow lines. *E.M.Johnson*

Fallowfield Station, May 6th.1956: Class A5 Tank No.**69815** hurries through a clean and tidy-looking Fallowfield Station with the 9.30 a.m. Liverpool to Hull Boat Train. Despite its origin, the train will have travelled into Manchester Central prior to reversing for this, the second leg of its journey. The A5 will come off at Guide Bridge where an electric locomotive will whisk the train over and through the Pennines to Sheffield Victoria. From this point eastwards steam traction will, once again, be in charge. *A.C.Gilbert*

Fallowfield Station, Summer 1980: The station survives, just, though much dilapidation has occured in the intervening twenty-four years. Notice the truncated passage of the former Down line and the heavily overgrown Up platform. The sidings survived for a while as a terminal for traffic from the London Brick Company. Like so much freight traffic, however, this was lost by the railways and the yard fell into subsequent disuse. *Raymond Keeley*

Site of Fallowfield Station, May 1st.1994: Fallowfield Station closed to passengers on July 7th.1958: yet the line was to linger as an alternative to the route into Piccadilly for another thirty years. The last passenger train, a Sunday morning diverted Sheffield-Liverpool, passed through on January 10th.1988. On October 15th. of that year the very last train-the diverted 15.54 Trafford Park to Southampton Freightliner-rumbled under Wilmslow Road, past the ruined platforms and all life here had ceased. Track lifting commenced in September 1991 consigning this once-fine stretch of railway into wasteful oblivion. As we ponder on this present-day wilderness we should reflect and consider the sad withering of assets: a fine stretch of double track alignment runing through high density housing and offering connections between major centres-all lain now to rack and ruin. *E.M.Johnson*

Godley Junction, December 29th.1967: Before the demise of steam, and the closure of the Woodhead route in particular, Godley Junction was the scene of intense activity. With freight interchange sidings handling vast quantities of Trans-Pennine movements, especially coal from the Yorkshire pits, Godley, housed engine turning facilities, and a water tower. Here was the spot where a major route westwards began: the CLC's line across Cheshire and South Manchester to Glazebrook en route to the Atlantic port of Liverpool and the point of interchange between electric and steam traction for west-bound freight. As steam ends its final full year of operation on British Railways 8F 2-8-0 No.**48317** pulls out of Brookfold Sidings, along the Through Siding, before being turned out onto the Down line towards Apethorn Junction, on the south-east side of Godley Station, with a Northwich-bound coal train. Heading along the former CLC line towards Apethorn and Woodley, the train will travel via Stockport Tiviot Dale, Cheadle Junction, Northenden and Skelton Junction before taking the former Cheshire Midland line via Hale towards Northwich.

John Clarke, courtesy Museum of Science & Industry in Manchester.

Godley East, March 29th.1994: Few illustrations show better the demise of freight traffic on the British railway system than this. Just under twenty-seven years separate the two pictures; in the meantime Godley Junction has wasted away to become a mere staging post, now known as "Godley East", on the rump of a once great trunk railway. The high-rise flats of neighbouring Hattersley provide a landmark for comparisons. The observant reader may just be able to discern the lofty yard lamp post-peeping through the flourishing thicket on the right-hand side of the picture. *E.M.Johnson*

Godley Junction, November 10th.1984: Three major changes have now contrived to reduce Godley's status: Steam has gone from British Railways, the Woodhead route has closed and the CLC line via Apethorn and Woodley to Stockport Tiviot Dale has faded into oblivion-witness the overgrown remains of the pointwork on the right-hand side of the view. The Class 506 1500v dc EMUs now ply the tip of the former Great Central main line as far as Hadfield and round to Glossop. One week later, this set will be withdrawn and after the 7th. of December the route will be re-electrified at 25kv ac, bringing it into line with the remainder of the electrified routes in and out of Manchester Piccadilly and taking away one of the last vestiges of separate identity on the former Eastern Region side of the station. *Timothy Grimshaw*

Godley East, March 29th.1994: Only the vast width of wasted catenary and two heaps of stone reveal this to be the same point from a mere ten years ago. Standardisation now rules in the form of 25 kv ac stock as Class **305 509** runs towards Godley East forming an afternoon train from Glossop to Manchester Piccadilly. Today, Godley East is beyond even its former pale shadow; closure and transfer of all services to the new Godley Station, further west and nearer to the centre of Godley itself, looks almost inevitable. *E.M.Johnson*

Between Godley and Newton, November 11th 1954: The most significant piece of railway development in the North West in the mid-1950s was undoubtedly the Manchester-Sheffield-Wath electrification scheme primarily involving the former Great Central main line between Manchester London Road and Sheffield Victoria. Completed in June, 1954 this was to be the first U.K. main line where all express, freight and local traffic was handled by electric traction. To handle express passenger trains seven Co-Co locomotives of 2,700 h.p. were built at Gorton Works in 1954. Exemplifying operation on the "Woodhead" line, as it was known, is one such locomotive-No.**27003** at the head of a 7-coach Sheffield-Manchester express moving swiftly and silently along just west of Godley station. *B.K.B.Green*

Between Godley Station and Newton, March 29th.1994: Some forty years separate these two views. The slopes of the cutting are thick now with foliage, houses are springing up along the lineside and continuously-welded rail is the order of things. In the meantime, Manchester-Sheffield trains have gone from the Woodhead line and now traverse the former Midland line-the "Hope Valley" route between Hazel Grove and Sheffield Midland. The overhead catenary now hums with current at 25 kv and powers the 304 and 305 EMUs between Manchester Piccadilly and Glossop/Hadfield. **305 504** forming an afternoon train to Glossop slows preparatory to a stop at Godley Station, a new venture hard by Mottram Road (A57). The old Godley Station now being re-designated "Godley East." *E.M.Johnson*

The name "Guide Bridge" will mean little to enthusiasts outside of the Greater Manchester. Guide Bridge itself is actually a district of nearby Ashton-under-Lyne, nowadays part of what is termed "The Metropolitan Borough of Tameside." Situated on the eastern side of Manchester, Guide Bridge is, or rather was, at a confluence of an assortment of railway lines yielding a plethora of traffic movements. Principal amongst these was its position as an important calling point on the former Great Central main line from Manchester to Sheffield. The LNWR had interests here and ran a direct line from Stockport via Reddish and Denton (Q.V.) Stalybridge, for traffic to Huddersfield and Leeds, was on a direct route from Guide Bridge and the station saw traffic from a one-time independent local line: the Oldham, Ashton and Guide Bridge Railway (O.A.& G.B.) A short distance away was Ashton Moss where access to the L&Y's "Ashton Branch" from Stalybridge existed. Ashton Moss was also the site of a large freight interchange sidings where trans-Pennine freight was made up and dispatched. Indeed, Guide Bridge in its heyday had been something of a microcosm of northern industry: collieries, a considerable number of cotton mills, electrical and general engineering workshops, a gas engine factory and, a little local peculiarity-a sewing machine factory; all stood cheek-by-jowl with iron foundries, and a sewage works. Working around the clock to interface with all these was the railway, dominating the landscape and laced around the place like a rather more intricate version of a spider's web.

Guide Bridge

Guide Bridge, looking east-early 1950s: An "opposite hand" view to that showing No.**61162**; this picture shows the scene from the end of the station looking towards Dukinfield-home of the Great Central's carriage and wagon works. On offer is a delightful antiquity: the two-coach push-pull set which plied between Glossop and Manchester London Road. Hauled by C13 4-4-2 tank No.**67438** this unit comprised an ex-Great Central 50' clerestory and a 12-wheeled Saloon. The two-storey building behind the locomotive was a goods shed, visible to the side is the southern tip of the Brookside siding complex referred to previously. The lattice bridge spanning the tracks ran from the bank of the Manchester and Ashton-under-Lyne canal across to Bridge Street. *Author's Collection*

Guide Bridge, March 29th.1994: The term "push-pull" is no longer extant in railway terminology, though, of course, electrical multiple-unit and much express stock is propelled that way nowadays. The same lattice footbridge and overhead catenary supports frame today's scene at the east end of the station as **158763** sweeps round from the Stalybridge line forming the 13.05 service from Newcastle to Liverpool Lime Street.
E.M. Johnson.

Guide Bridge Station, 1930s: Two pairs of tracks ran through the station here, quadruple track stretching from Ardwick to Hyde Junction. At neighbouring Fairfield Junction a branch from Manchester Central via Fallowfield joined the Sheffield line from London Road. Known as the Manchester Central Station Railway this nine and three-quarter mile line had given the Great Central access to another Manchester terminal as well as a direct route to Liverpool-which city it then gained via the metals of the CLC. By the looks of things "Director" 4-4-0 No.**5503** *Somme* has come off the Fallowfield line at Fairfield with an Up express and has run along the Up Slow lines into Guide Bridge station. A 1930s view packed with atmosphere, this is still a scene firmly rooted in the pre-Group era: a magnificent Great Central engine, teak-bodied coaching stock, the famous lattice-post semaphores and wooden-bodied wagons from Bolsover Collieries. *Collection of R.K.Blencowe*

Guide Bridge, March 29th.1994: Though the platform buildings on the south side of the station survive, they are now boarded-up, empty, cheerless brick vaults void of both soul, staff and passengers. Now the platforms in front stand trackless and crumbling and the bustle of activity that surrounded the arrival of "Somme" has long vanished. *E.M.Johnson*

Norbury Viaduct-Buxton Road-August 1900: One of a series of official views commissioned by the Midland Railway prior to the opening of their New Mills and Heaton Mersey line in 1902. The Norbury Viaduct, at 240 yards, spans the Buxton Road (numbered 20), open land (21) and the Macclesfield Road (22). Construction is a combination of brick arches, 11 in number and each 33'-3$^{7}/_{8}$" wide, and an early type of steel parapet girder. This span covers 54'-0" square and 120'-0" on the skew.

Though this book offers many harsh contrasts between the old and the new orders, I find this picture particularly poignant, contrasting as it does two totally different worlds. On the one hand we look upon a sleepy, rural Cheshire at the end of the Victorian era. The Great War was still fourteen years away, the Buxton Road yet a cobbled highway with horse-drawn traffic still the main mode of transport. Overhead, one of the last great thrusting enterprises of the Midland Railway has not yet seen its first train. It hardly seems possible that such a world could change so dramatically. *R.J.Essery Collection*

Bridge 20, June 4th.1994: Today we see the same structure striding over the A6-a highway now positively teeming with road traffic. What a vast array of social and economic changes divides the people of 1900 from those 94 years on! Notice the north-bound lorry carrying stone on the left: a vehicle count on this road has shown no less than 92 such vehicles passing along in a space of less than one hour. One wonders how much longer the famed former ICI "Hoppers" will rumble overhead before succumbing to the all-pervading "market forces" philosophy.

E.M.Johnson

Heald Green, February 12th.1958: The Styal Line, the LNWR's Wilmslow and Levenshulme Railway, was used as something of a proving ground for the Manchester-Crewe 25kV electrification scheme. All this generated great interest among us enthusiasts of the time-something of a climax being reached when the pioneer 25kV electric loco, the converted Western Region Gas Turbine engine No.E1000, arrived at East Didsbury in the Autumn of 1959. However, the old order still ruled at Heald Green a year earlier when the wiring team was busily erecting the catenary on the Down line. Note that both the contact and earth lines are suspended by temporary hooks, the fittings from the masts have yet to be installed. Semaphore signals remain for the time being, but these will soon be gone, their place taken by the inevitable multiple aspect colour lights. The wiring train locomotive, an ex-LNWR 0-8-0 No.**49394** had started life in 1901 as a four cylinder Compound and was later rebuilt as a Simple engine with a Belpaire firebox to Class G2a. A "no frills", rugged design, these engines were to be seen at work on both through and local workings on the Styal line. The last one was withdrawn in 1964. The LNWR timber buildings here dated from the opening of the line 1910 and held sway until their replacement in 1959 by thoroughly modern-looking steel, glass and brick structures. The concrete footbridge, a new addition, has yet to be commissioned; two platform seats are acting as impromptu barriers! Notice the men on the roof of the wiring train-despite the limited clearance beneath the bridge there is not a "hard hat" to be seen and neither of the men on the track wear yellow vests-interesting sidelights on "safe practice." *British Railways*

Heald Green

Heald Green, July 21st.1994: It is hard to believe that over thirty six years separate these two views. Electric services between Manchester and Crewe began on September 27th.1960, a date I remember well as I had the distinction of being the first fare-paying passenger! Trains between Manchester Airport and beyond now give Heald Green its best service ever: seen departing is the four-coach 08.57 Airport-Blackpool train made up of two Diesel-powered Class 156 units. The attractive young lady sat on the Up platform was en route to Wilmslow and provides an interesting comment on today's Styal Line workings. With most trains turning off further down the line to Manchester Airport, she had a lengthy wait but had patiently asked the guard of each incoming train "is this one for Wilmslow?" Perhaps a case for more "customer" information? *E.M.Johnson*

Heaton Norris, April 26th.1956: Heaton Norris holds a special place in the annals of Stockport's railway history. The town's first station opened here on June 4th. 1840 on the first section of the Manchester and Birmingham Railway. An impressive goods warehouse, just out of sight on the left and fronting on to Wellington Road (the A6) was opened by the LNWR in 1882 to cater for Stockport's considerable cotton traffic. Seen from Bowerfold Lane, and looking south towards the viaduct, "Princess Royal" Pacific No.**46203** *Princess Margaret Rose* gets into her stride on the last leg of her journey northwards with a Euston to Manchester London Road express. Heaton Norris station can just be glimpsed behind the colour light signals. The yard on the right once served the S&T Department and also serviced a timber works; notice the two former Midland Railway clerestory coaches-probably doing duty as mess vans. *Tom Lewis*

Scene from Bowerfold Lane, July 18th.1994: *Princess Margaret Rose* was withdrawn from service in April 1963 after a period in store and survives, happily, as a working locomotive. The LNWR goods warehouse, a Grade II Listed Building, now does duty for Messrs.Bryant as a storage depot and "Airpark". The track layout here has been altered radically since the days of steam; no trace survives of Heaton Norris station, closed long ago-on March 2nd.1959. The S&T depot has gone too-though the ground to the right still bears the impression of sleepers. On a bright sunny summer's day Class **90 005** accelerates past the former goods warehouse at the head of the 10.00 London Euston to Manchester Piccadilly. Locomotive-hauled trains are fast becoming a rarity on today's railway, here as elesewhere: in a spell of 1½ hours at Heaton Norris this was one of just two such trains that appeared! *E.M.Johnson*

Hyde Central. September 9th 1966. This short section of the former Great Central & Midland Joint line was still witnessing its fair share of freight traffic although local goods workings had finished some months earlier. Having recently been transferred to Heaton Mersey, 8F No.**48365** takes its turn on one of the many short workings that were a familiar pattern for the area. Dewsnap to Gowhole, back to Heaton Mersey, trip working to Godley Junction, and so on. Platform level at Hyde Central was attained via a three storey climb from the Great Norbury Street entrance, an almost ecclesiastical frontage of massive proportions for a small town station. *K. Rathbone.*

Hyde Central. August 1994. The Down side waiting shelter has survived to give the remaining patrons of the Rose Hill to Manchester trains a more than adequate protection in this view towards Hyde Junction. *E.M. Johnson.*

Levenshulme Station, pre-WWI: A plain, starkly-worded hoarding leaves the intending traveller in no doubt as to their whereabouts. One of a tiny handful of photographs which have survived to show us just how our local stations looked in this, the heyday of the railway. Standing on the corner of Albert Road, at its junction with Marshall Road, we gaze on Levenshulme Station and, with it, a slice of history. The station had opened as far back as 1854, replacing a halt further down the line at a place known as "Rushford." The scene here is pure Edwardiana: a horse and waiting carriage pass the time of day just below the steps up to the booking office, a lady with a bonnet passes by, the sun shines and the shops protect their wares with the customary striped sunblinds. Here and there ornate gas lamps hang, their mantled, gently hissing, yellow light casting eerie shadows on to flagged pavements when the sun sets on this scene. *Collection of G.K.Fox*

Levenshulme

Levenshulme Station, 28th.March 1994: A bustling Levenshulme, still with its station-alive and staffed! Latter-day economies in maintenance have forced the railway authorities to remove the upper storey on the Down side of the line. The single-arched bridge was replaced in 1948 with the present steel and concrete structure; this was to enable Manchester Corporation to run double-decker buses along Albert Road. The contract for replacement was let to Thomas Wrigley of Manchester. Now what a contrast elsewhere! Sedate, walled fronts to the shops on Albert Road have given way to the arrival of the brash-fronted fast-food outlets lending a similar, somewhat stereotyped look to almost every high street in the land. On a further point of railway interest, Herbert William Garratt the famous inventor and patentee of the Garratt articulated locomotive, moved with his family to No.20 Albert Road in November, 1907. Here he established an office and worked in close conjunction with the world-famous locomotive building firm of Beyer, Peacock& Co. just a few miles away in Gorton. *E.M.Johnson*

Levenshulme South Station, Pre First War: Levenshulme, once a small borough independent of Manchester, had two railway stations. The second, on the A6 near to the boundary with Heaton Chapel, was opened on May 2nd.1892 when the Manchester, Sheffield and Lincolnshire Railway's Manchester Central Station Railway from Fairfield to Chorlton opened for traffic. (The first section, from Chorlton to Fallowfield, had opened the previous year). Our scene is pure history book stuff: outside the station a gaggle of children stare across a quiet road at the photographer. Come darkness, ornate gas lamps will light the way as prospective travellers pass by poster boards headed "GCR" and cross the parquet floor to the booking office. In the middle of the road an aproned shop assistant pauses as the open-topped tramcar hums and rattles its way past en route to neighbouring Stockport. Horse droppings litter the highway, cloth-capped men, their womenfolk at their side, saunter by-a seemingly unhurried, tranquil world. *Collection of G.K.Fox*

Levenshulme South Station buildings, April 17th.1994: Levenshulme lost its other railway station on and from July 3rd.1958 when the passenger service beteen Manchester Central and Guide Bridge was withdrawn. In the interim, the buildings became a DIY shop, the title of which became the more politically correct "Home Improvement Centre" as seen here. Dereliction ruled the day when I paused to take this picture. The shop premises were empty, the building boarded over and all seemed set for demolition. Happily, in the interim, developers have done a magnificent job in rebuilding the facade to an exact replica of the former MS&L structure. Sadly, below the road the railway has long gone-the last train ran in October 1988-the shallow cutting having become an impromptu dumping ground in the meantime. Beneath the tarmac of the 1990s the cobbled roadway and the tramlines lie buried; the children became war heroes, war widows and yesterday's old-age pensioners. Minus horses and trams this is today's Levenshulme. *E.M.Johnson*

Manchester Central, March 30th.1962: A bright, clear Spring day sees BR Standard Class 5 4-6-0 No.**73002** pulling briskly away from platform 8 with a stopping train bound for Sheffield (Midland) over the Dore and Chinley (Hope Valley) line. Across on platform 6, beneath a myriad of cast iron scrollwork, a train of main line stock has arrived; almost certainly an express from, or to, St.Pancras.
W.D.Cooper

G - Mex

G-Mex Centre, March 30th.1994: It was fortunate indeed that the shell of Manchester's Central station was saved from ruin. Though the demise and closure of almost any part of the rail network is to be regretted, at least future generations can admire this splendid Victorian architectural masterpiece which now functions as an exhibition and events centre. Lorries and trailers are now scattered over a sea of tarmac and white lines; the awnings, platforms and the thunder of trains are but a memory. *E.M.Johnson*

Manchester Central

Manchester Central, May 14th.1959: "Royal Scot" No.**46122** *Royal Ulster Rifleman* looks smart and pristine alongside platform 4 with an express for St.Pancras. The "Scots" were late arrivals on this section of the Midland line and had but a brief reign before being supplanted by Type 4 Diesels; "Britannia" Pacifics having taken the lead in the interim. Over on platform 9, Ivatt 2-6-2 tank No.**41232** blows off whilst awaiting departure with a local.
J.A.Peden

Manchester London Road, Summer 1937: Four minutes to two, the Union Flag flies high over the splendid building of 1865 designed by Mills and Murgatroyd. Austin taxis line up for business and the approach is thronged with passengers. This is Coronation year, soon Britain will have a new King and Queen and everyone hopes the sun will continue to shine. *G.K.Fox Collection*

Manchester London Road, Winter 1960: These were trying times for rail travellers. Amidst the half-demolished Victorian frontage and the embryo tower block was a mass of scaffolding, planked walkways and canvas screens. Just outside the station can be seen the temporary booking offices that did duty amidst the transitory structures. Bemused passengers could choose a cheap trip to Leeds-departures Wednesdays and Saturdays-for 7/3d. London, with a choice of routes still on offer, could be reached for 42/-. Through electric services, though, were still a full six years away. *Harry Bedford*

Manchester Piccadilly, March 30th.1994: The new station has since celebrated its 33rd.birthday and this is how it looks today. The only tangible evidence of yesteryear's station can be glimpsed above the Centreline bus: the top of the arc of the Victorian trainshed roof. Piccadilly in the last decade of the 20th.century is a thriving, bustling place. Notice the Union Flag still flies; now we are on the eve of a new era, for this week the nation's railways will embark on their transition back to a form of private ownership. And this is where we came in..... *E.M.Johnson*

Manchester Piccadilly

Manchester London Road

Manchester London Road Station, viewed from Whitworth Street, 1960: "THIS LUXURY STATION WILL GIVE A NEW LOOK TO LONDON ROAD AND PROVIDE GREATLY IMPROVED FACILITIES FOR THE NEW ELECTRIC SERVICES COMMENCING SEPTEMBER 1960." So reads the sign fixed to the wall below the station approach as the myriad of steel girders form slowly and inexorably into the space-age structure that became Rail House. Alongside this rising edifice, the Victorian remains of the 1860s booking hall and offices remain in limbo-Messrs.Connell and Finnigan still have a substantial demolition job to do. *British Railways*

Manchester Piccadilly, March 30th.1994: Rail House is now a well-known landmark, as familiar today as its smoke-blackened nineteenth century predecessor was yesterday. Across the road the fire station has long gone and today's cars race along Whitworth Street and round the one-way system into Aytoun Street with ever-increasing speed. Coming up behind, a number 192 bus from the newly-inaugurated "Stagecoach" service between Manchester and Hazel Grove rounds the corner-a stark contrast to the gentle swishing sound of the 218 and 219 trolleybuses that passed this way some thirty-five years ago. Any minute now a Metrolink tram will sweep down from Aytoun Street and disappear into the hole in the wall that once formed the entrance to the goods depot -now transformed into the Metrolink terminus. Electric services really have come to town *E.M.Johnson*

Manchester Piccadilly, September 1960: One of a series of official views taken to show the completion of the station rebuilding immediately prior to the inauguration of electric services to Crewe later that month. Though the loss of the fine Victorian frontage and booking hall can only be regretted, it has to be said that the new station was light, airy and clean-even if the result, as with the new Euston, was something more akin to an airport than the traditional appearace of a large railway station. One assumes the photographer was up with the lark to catch the concourse almost devoid of passengers.
British Railways

Manchester Piccadilly, March 30th.1994: The concourse looks even more like an airline terminal now. A later re-modelling scheme has further removed the traditional railway station image. Smart-looking shops have sprung up alongside the various spots where ticket collectors gathered and clipped their little slips of paper and card in the teeming thousands. Piccadilly, like many main-line termini is now an "open" station. This is the day and age of the sell-off, with railway premises seen as fair game for whatever commercial enterprise best makes money. Future historians may scrutinise the front cover of the young man's Sun newspaper: "Stand Down" reads the banner headline, but the reader appears intent on other matters. *E.M.Johnson*

Manchester London Road, c.1951: London Road Station prior to around 1958/59 was a vastly different place to the station we know as Piccadilly today. This is a view taken from the old Down MSJ&A platform on the station's south-east flank above Fairfield Street. Looking across to the Up platform we take in 3F 0-6-0 No.**43717** and its train of three brake vans, a horsebox and a petrol tanker waiting for the road before moving off in the direction of Ardwick and Longsight, in transit from, possibly, one of the Salford yards. Behind the railing was platform 7; the ex-Great Central platforms, on the station's far side, were lettered A-C to avoid confusion with those of the ex-LMS which were numbered from 1 upwards. Just to further confuse matters, there was no platform 2 at London Road in those days! This had disappeared in an earlier rebuilding programme. *Fred Walton*

Manchester Piccadilly, March 30th.1994: Principal amongst the features of the London Road rebuilding programme of the late 1950s was the provision of a lengthy island platform on the site of those of the former MSJ&AR. Despite this though, through electric running from Altrincham and onwards to Crewe, had to wait until 1970 when the Altrincham lines were re-wired and energised on the common 25kV AC. With the advent of the very successful Metrolink LRT system, through running to Altrincham has ended and the local electric service now terminates at Deansgate. In the Autumn of 1988 Piccadilly Station was altered ("re-modelled") yet again with, amongst other things, a further lengthening of platforms 13 and 14. An early afternoon Liverpool-Newcastle service, formed by **158854**, starts away-providing an interesting contrast with the motive power in our scene of some 40 years ago. The completely re-modelled track layout makes direct comparison with the earlier view difficult: as a rough guide the alignment of the tracks where the 3F was waiting are now covered by the present platform 12-to the immediate right of the 158 DMU. *E.M.Johnson*

Mauldeth Road, May 15th.1957: "Coronation" Class Pacific No.**46240** *City of Coventry* rolls in to Mauldeth Road station with an early evening stopping train from Manchester London Road to Crewe. Fresh from an overhaul at Crewe Works, lightly loaded local trips such as this, provided a good opportunity for engines to be "run in" before transfer back to the home shed-in this case 1B, Camden. Such sights, with engines looking in pristine condition, provided a bonus for enthusiasts as well as enabling the engines to be seen in what were otherwise unfamilair surroundings. Mauldeth Road, with its LNWR-style wooden buildings and platforms is seen little altered from the opening of the Styal line in 1910. *City of Coventry* was withdrawn in September, 1964. The wooden platforms, signal box and semaphores were all swept away in the Manchester-Crewe electrification programme of 1958-60. The station suffered a final humiliation when the remaining LNWR buildings (on the Down platform) were destroyed in an arson attack at the end of October 1985. *R.E.Gee*

Mauldeth Road

Mauldeth Road, March 5th.1994: A born-again Mauldeth Road now sees express passenger traction in a somewhat different guise. Winter afternoon sun shines as Class **158805** unit flashes through forming the 11.28 Scarborough to Manchester Airport service. No wooden-bodied vans assemble now behind the Up platform; the goods yard and embankment here was removed in recent years to make way for a B&Q superstore and car park. Notice the long concrete platforms: now out of bounds to passengers and part of ambitious plans for longer trains which never materialised. *E.M.Johnson*

Oxford Road, September 17th.1958: A view looking towards All Saints close by the junction with Wakefield Street; Station Approach is off to the right, to the side of the photographer. The line of the former MSJ&A between what was then London Road and Oxford Road stations was to play a key role in the Manchester-Crewe electrification programme-then beginning to march inexorably forward. Several bridges had to be replaced, this bridge, with cast iron girders, was to be substituted by a reinforced concrete structure. A striking contrast, but as of nothing compared to the metamorphosis that Oxford Road Station itself was to undergo. As with other pictures in this series the contemporary street scene takes centre stage with road vehicles making interesting character studies. A Ford Consul heads the traffic stream followed by a Ford Prefect seen overtaking a Leyland Tiger bus belonging to the North Western Road Car Company; an Austin A35 trails behind. The mighty red-brick Refuge Assurance building, just visible on the left and hard by the railway, provides an interesting landmark. Of less stature, but providing a valuable public service was the famous Oxford Surgical Store; next door, Halon tailor's shop, complete with white pull-out blinds looks almost quaint now. Guinness, still heavily advertised today, was always a novel user of advertising jargon; lower down, above the Ford Zephyr, yet another drink advert tempts the Mancunian thirst! *British Railways*

Oxford Road, March 30th.1994: A surprisingly quiet moment in today's world of hustle and bustle; yet this was 10.15 on a normal weekday and presents a scene little different from almost thirty-six years ago. Our focal point, the single-arched underbridge, has long been replaced by the reinforced concrete structure that now spans Oxford Road. The buildings on the immediate left-hand side have changed little; although the Refuge Assurance Company have now deserted their lofty vault-like building for more modern premises outside Wilmslow in leafy Cheshire. Messrs.Halon still have their tailor's shop beyond the bridge; but the famous surgical shop has moved and the BBC studios now occupy the site further down Oxford Road. *E.M.Johnson*

Deansgate, Knott Mill end, 15th.November 1956: A schoolboy conundrum of the 1920s asked: "where can you cross Deansgate without walking over the tram lines?" The answer to that question is contained here in this interesting and now historic view. Standing on Deansgate we are looking towards Knott Mill with the bridge carrying the approach tracks into Manchester Central in front of us. Along from here can be seen two more bridges: both these carry the MSJ&A Railway, Knott Mill and Deansgate station is off to the left, just out of sight on the corner of Whitworth Street West. Just here, beneath the first arch is Deansgate, the second carries the railway over Chester Road where the trams continued on to Old Trafford, Stretford, Sale and Altrincham. By today's standards the road is quiet, a solitary Ford Zephyr is parked to one side-no yellow lines to worry motorists then! Tucked in front of the main line bridge Messrs.Gilbert & Quinn-"Used Commercial Sales" and "Cars Purchased for Cash" carry on business. Behind the MSJ&A bridge are Black and Decker and Messrs.Rootes Driving School. By Whitworth Street West a corner pub advertises Higson's Ales and an RAC sign points motorists to Manchester Airport-then but a pale shadow of the empire it has become. Auto Glass Supplies stands in between the two bridges with hoardings proclaiming the varying pleasures of beer (when did Mancunians ever need reminding of that tipple?!), Digger Flake tobacco, the Library Theatre and The Hippodrome at Ardwick Green: take your pick!

British Railways

Deansgate

Deansgate, Knott Mill end, March 27th.1994: Despite being a very busy thoroughfare, we are able to view Deansgate in a quiet moment in this mid-morning study. After an absence of some twenty-four years it is good to see a form of rail traffic using the former CLC bridge. Pedestrians on Deansgate can now walk UNDER the tram lines! The refurbishment and cleaning programme in the Castlefield area has left its mark on the structure-turning it into something of a focal point. Gilbert & Quinn have long vacated the premises immediately in front of the bridge; these are now the home of Messrs.Bauer Millett, this particular showroom specialising in the famous Harley-Davidson American motorcycles; in 1956 who would have imagined it possible to pay over £10,000 for a mere motorbike?! *E.M.Johnson*

Pendlebury, view from footpath off Bolton Road, looking to Brindle Heath, July 28th.1961: Class 5 No.**45295** heads west towards Swinton and Moorside with an 8-coach express. The train is on the Down Fast line and will have travelled over Brindle Heath via the flyover referred to previously. The tracks on the left are the Slow lines which curve away towards Agecroft Junction past the colliery on the left-hand side. Notice the crossovers enabling traffic to pass from Slow to Fast lines and vice-versa controlled by the appropriate semaphores. The Distant arms are for Pendlebury box, closed on May 22nd.1966. Pendlebury station, out of sight behind the photographer, closed on October 3rd.1960. *W.D.Cooper*

From footpath off Bolton Road, July 26th.1994: Precisely why so many trees and shrubs flourish alongside railways today is not completely clear. Whether soot and sulphur emissions from generations of steam locomotives kept foliage at bay cannot be established: certainly, lineside fires are no longer commonplace and they, inevitably, kept down saplings and grass. Traversing the former Slow lines is **150136** forming a morning service from Southport. The Manchester city skyline appears through the dull haze of a sultry summer day. *E.M.Johnson*

Approaches to Romiley Junction, c.1964: Three lines converged at Romiley: left to right, these were: Midland Railway towards Bredbury Junction, sometimes known as the "Marple Curve" and opened in 1875, the centre line-Great Central & Midland Joint line via Reddish and Belle Vue to Ashburys, and thirdly-just visible in the top right-hand corner, the Sheffield & Midland Joint line via Hyde Junction into Manchester London Road. Coming up the Midland line is Class 5 No.**44708** with a 4-coach stopping train via Stockport Tiviot Dale to Sheffield. It was at this point that the train was entering the Engineer's District of Derby North-a relic of former Midland Railway practice which did not end until 1966. *John Fairclough*

Romiley

Approach to Romiley Junction, August 13th.1994: A vast overgrowth of trees makes present-day comparison virtually impossible-certainly from the photographic viewpoint. The curve down to Bredbury Junction was taken out of use in 1967-although a single line remained in situ into the 1970s pending possible re-instatement. On the former Great Central & Midland line, a two-car Metro-Cammell DMU **101660** slows for the junction forming a morning service from Manchester Piccadilly to Marple. The former Marple curve is under siege from encraoching foliage and vegetation to the left. The Hyde line has, likewise, disappeared from view. *E.M.Johnson*

Railway Hotel, Stockport c.1948: Along with patron saints, lambs, lions, and various mythical creatures, the name "Railway" seems to have been a popular and well-loved title for what must be hundreds of English pubs. The Railway Hotel on Wellington Road North, Stockport-just across from the junction with Georges Road-is well-placed to earn its title. The LNWR's Manchester to Crewe line passes just behind the photographer before striding over the Mersey on Stockport's famous 27-arched viaducts. Down the road was the CLC's Wellington Road goods depot which fanned out at Georges Road Junction on the Godley to Glazebrook line; this, at one time a most intensively-worked freight route, burrowed deep through a man-made sandstone cleft before tunnelling into Tiviot Dale station. William HT Crick was the Licensee, and Wilson's ("the sign of quality"), along with Bass draught and in bottle, was the brew on offer here when this picture was taken. An almost cottage-like white appearance offers a contrast between The Railway and the terraced houses next door. The A6 is still cobbled, a feature shared with many streets in this part of the world just after the War; overhead, the electric wires betray the existence of trams. Stockport's red and white vehicles outlived their Manchester brethren, surviving until August 1951. *Collection of R.P.Hepner*

Stockport

Railway Hotel, March 28th.1994: Messrs.Greenalls now own the familiar hostelry on Wellington Road North and Wyatt Street, running alongside, has become a cul-de-sac. The cobbles lie buried beneath the tarmac of the A6, along with the rails that bore the trams to shake and rattle past the front door. Notice the proliferation of cars; a degree of patience was needed to catch a moment free of traffic on a busy Monday morning. Eventually, one arose: it lasted a bare 1/125th of a second! "The Railway", some forty-six years on, with Mr.Austin James Flood as the licensee, still looks a pleasant place: I wonder if the beer tastes the same? *E.M.Johnson*

Rochdale Station, June 3rd.1965: Rivalling Wigan as probably the best known of the Lancashire Cotton Mill towns, Rochdale has a proud heritage. The Gothic Town Hall, Gracie Fields and Sir Cyril Smith number amongst its notabilities. Not to be outdone by the municipal authorities, the Lancashire & Yorkshire Railway provided this splendid frontage when the new station was opened in March 1889. This magnificent glass and steel canopy, once housing a splendid clock tower, was just part of the splendour. The BR maroon enamelled sign, the parcels delivery van and the now anachronistic-looking "KEEP LEFT" signs all put this picture firmly rooted in the past.

British Railways

Rochdale Station, August 11th.1994: In the last thirty years British Rail have had more than their fair share of problems. Not the least of these has been the maintenance of an often crumbling Victorian infrastructure on a sometimes limited budget. Whatever the architectural merits or de-merits of the new frontage, provided in 1980, the building must be easier to look after and the station today is reasonably bright and clean. Sadly, the glory of the pre-Group L&Y Railway is somehow lacking.

E.M.Johnson

Salford Goods Yard

Perhaps more than anything else, the loss of freight traffic from today's railway presents us with the biggest single change of scene. Though many of the great Victorian passenger terminals survive, albeit in somewhat altered form, they are, in essence, extant. The same cannot be said for goods facilities. Until the 1960s there existed throughout the land and in every great city a number of goods depots and adjacent yards. At some point, now thirty years or more past, decline and then decay set in as changing patterns of freight operation took over and more and more goods traffic moved across to road haulage.

Even today, vast hulks of buildings and acres of land still lie derelict and stagnant; their primary purpose long gone, they linger like some mummified dinosaur-relics of a distant age and a different era. From Manchester, we cross the River Irwell, that historic navigable waterway, into Salford to look at one such feature: the yards and depots known variously as Irwell Street, Salford Goods and Bailey Yard.

Salford's passenger station had opened in 1838: in May, 1844, the Liverpool and Manchester Railway opened a short line from Ordsall Lane, in Salford, to Victoria Station. This line, built on a brick viaduct no more than 32 feet high, formed the outline shape of what eventually became Salford goods yard.

The yard, or rather yards, was spread over a considerable area. Bounded on the north-east side by New Bailey Street, on the south-east by the railway into Victoria Station, and on the south-west by the Manchester, Bolton and Bury Canal and Oldfield Road. Goods facilities at Salford had expanded steadily with the inexorable growth of the nineteenth century railway; by the late 1860s further expansion was only possible in an easterly direction. This lay over the ground occupied by the New Bailey Prison. A grim edifice by today's standards, the Prison had opened in 1790 and was extended in 1815. Housing some 700 inmates, it had been described as one of the best regulated institutions in the country. The New Bailey Prison closed in 1868 when Strangeways opened its doors. It was on this site that the Lancashire & Yorkshire Railway built the New Bailey warehouse. Opening in 1872, the warehouse contained 12 roads and a 10-ton overhead travelling crane. As ever with such premises, further expansion was needed, but in broad outline, the Salford and New Bailey yards were complete.

Salford Goods Yard, February 27th.1960: A picture showing something of the vast size of the complex, albeit now in a somewhat run-down state and in the last decade of its existence. In the background can be seen the low viaducts carrying the Manchester and Wigan and Manchester and Bolton lines of the former L&YR. These split at Windsor Bridge to travel via Pendleton with interconnections at Brindle Heath. The canopies of Salford Station, a three-platform affair and serving all four running lines can be seen clearly above the viaducts. Barking along, over the section known as the "Preston" yard, is an ex-L&Y saddletank 0-6-0 No.**51413**-withdrawn a year later. Lines from the New Bailey yard, off to the right, crossed Irwell Street, a continuation of New Quay Street-just beyond the famous Granada T.V.complex. An attempt by the L&Y in 1871 to stop up Irwell Street failed. Various short-wheelbase engines were used in the yard apart from these 0-6-0s: L&Y "Pug" 0-4-0s, LMS "Jinties" and Fowler 0-6-0 Dock Tanks all did their turns. *C.A.Appleton*

Salford

Salford Goods Yard, July 25th.1961: The weed-strewn state of the cobbled paving promotes an air of neglect as LMS "Jinty" 0-6-0 No.**47678** slogs along with a trainload of box vans. Acces to the running lines from the low-level yard was at Oldfield Road via a 1-in-27 incline-something a Yorkshire Engine 170 h.p. 0-4-0 Diesel, tried in 1962, reportedly did not take kindly to! *A.C.Gilbert*

New Bailey Yard, December 1940: Like so many cities, Salford and Manchester suffered badly from aerial bombardment in the Second War. The night of December 22nd.1940 was particularly onerous when bombs and thousands of incendiary devices pounded the two neighbours. Manchester's Exchange and Mayfield Stations suffered direct hits, cotton warehouses in the city centre were destroyed as well as the Free Trade Hall, though no doubt the obvious target was the adjacent Central Station. New Bailey Yard was hit by incendiary bombs and this rather mournful picture shows the blackened shells of the buildings and the orgy of destruction wrought by the Luftwaffe. Looking at the desolation, it is hard to believe the yard was put back into working order and lasted almost another quarter of a century.
Author's Collection

Site of Salford Goods Yard, from Stanley Street, July 14th.1994: Providing an amazing contrast with the 1960 view, this is Salford Irwell Street today. The yard had closed in the mid-1960s: New Bailey on March 23rd.1964, this section-Irwell Street-in August 1968. Long gone are the vans, the assortment of Tank engines that slogged over them for a century or more and the rails that bore them. Modern economics has put land in city centres at a premium and large, undeveloped patches, such as this, have been avidly snapped up for the inevitable car parking. The site today is known as Stanley Street Car Park, part of the NCP empire: how long this will last is hard to say as plans exist to build yet another road-a relief route between the A57 in Salford, at the junction of Regent Road and Water Street, along to join Trinity Way (A6042) linking with Great Ducie Street and Cheetham Hill Road. Salford Station, nowadays void of its canopies, still functions; though its neighbour, Salford Crescent takes the lion's share of passenger business in this area.
E.M.Johnson

Stalybridge, mid-1920s: Former LNWR "Experiment" Class No.**1002** *Warwickshire* awaits departure from the west end of the station with a stopping passenger train. The brake-ended coach, though of LNWR origin, is in the fully lined out early LMS livery. The splendidly proportioned 4-6-0 appears in the lined black livery of its parent company. The sight of a mill and associated chimneys serve as a reminder of the industrial heritage of this town that straggles the boundaries of industrial Lancashire and rural Cheshire. Stalybridge was a child of the Industrial Revolution. Cotton mills had arrived as far back as 1776 with Neddy Hall's Sootpoke mill in Rassbottom. The Globe iron works, belonging to one, John Summers, and sited just south of the station, began production in 1869. *P.F.Cooke*

Stalybridge,March 29th.1994: Much of Stalybridge's industry has departed; the four tracks between platforms 1 and 2 are reduced to two, and the station is now a mere staging post between Liverpool, Manchester, Huddersfield, Leeds and beyond. The Pennines are visible once again, something occasioned by the removal of the fine canopy of wood and iron, the mills and their slender, black-topped chimneys. In place of the rather charming *Warwickshire*, maroon-liveried coaching stock of a rather different kind-a Class 158 unit, wearing the West Yorkshire PTE livery-comes to a halt with the 12.32 service from Scarborough to Manchester Airport. *E.M.Johnson*

Stalybridge Station exterior viewed from Rasbottom Street, August 4th.1960: Stalybridge Station was a joint affair-owned by the London & North-Western and Great Central companies. This is the later building brought into use on May 21st.1885. An earlier station, a small terminus, owned by the Lancashire & Yorkshire Railway, closed in 1917. Here we view a handsome Victorian structure-with ornamental brickwork, handsome stone copings and a fully glazed canopy with elaborate cast iron supporting pillars. The slate-covered steeple is topped by an ornamental weather vane, a wonderful touch of Victorian artistry. Mr.F.Clarke was the Stationmaster in those days, when a cheap trip to Morecambe could be had for as little as 8/9d (44p). The sign adjacent to the station entrance warns: "all persons found tresspassing or loitering on these premises are liable to be taken into custody to be dealt with according to law." Stern stuff indeed.

British Railways

Stalybridge

Stalybridge Station exterior viewed from Rasbottom Street, March 29th.1994: The all-pervading car has taken the place of the splendid Victorian frontage and the prosaic corporate image logo surmounts a rather plain, uninviting entrance. A blank cement screed covers the wall where the fine buildings, once the province of cotton magnates and businessmen, stood. Whatever would the Victorians have thought?

E.M.Johnson

Electric services over the MSJ&A line began on May 10th.1931. A bold exercise and an act of faith in one of Manchester's busy suburban lines. The system chosen was 1500v Dc with overhead line contact-then designated as standard for future British practice. The intitials MSJ&AR became a catch phrase for: "many short journeys and absolute reliability"-a fair comment on what was an outstandingly successful venture. A timetable dated September 14th.1931 shows a service of no less than eighty-five trains provided between Manchester London Road and Altrincham: the first being at 6.25, the last at 11.45. A typical journey time was twenty-one minutes calling at all ten stations en route. Some trains, for example the 8.10 a.m. and 8.26 a.m. from London Road did the journey in fifteen and sixteen minutes respectively, though with only three intermediate stops in each case. The third class return fare from Manchester to Altrincham in those days was 9d.

Timperley

Between Brooklands and Timperley, 1930s: A scene that must have presented itself almost a million times over in the lifetime of the MSJ&A 1500v Dc electric units: one of the green-painted sets speeds alongside the Bridgewater Canal, through the former market garden district of Timperley en route for Altrincham. The LMS built these sets on 58 ft. underframes-an odd, and seemingly mysterious, departure from the 57 ft. otherwise extant. *G.H.Platt*

Timperley Station, 1930s: Aside from the regular and very punctual service of electric trains, the MSJ&A handled other passenger traffic. Services to Chester from Manchester Central were one example; another aspect was the train service from Manchester London Road to Liverpool Lime Street via Lymm and Warrington Bank Quay (Low-Level). Of the (then) four routes to Liverpool from Manchester this was undoubtedly the slowest and most tedious. The 1938 timetable shows a service taking up to 2 hours, 23 minutes for the 37¼ mile journey which involved no less than 22 stops! Typifying this leisurely meander of around sixty years ago, an unidentified Webb Coal Tank ambles into Timperley with its train of two coaches. The lofty bracket signal carries lower arms for the diverging route at Timperley Junction. Here a connecting curve ran off to join the Skelton Junction to Garston line at Broadheath Junction before proceeding through the Cheshire fields towards Lymm and Warrington. Services over this route came to an end on September 8th.1962. *G.H.Platt*

Timperley Junction, May 24th.1952: Former Great Central tank engines in the shape of the handsome and robust-looking C13 4-4-2s were a regular sight on Manchester Central to Chester trains in the mid-1950s. Seen approaching Timperley Junction, where the chord to Broadheath Junction curved away, is No.**67436** with an all stations stopping train to Chester Northgate. *R.E.Gee*

Approaching the site of Timperley Junction, July 13th.1994: An exact replica shot of the C13 picture is not possible nowadays: a small industrial estate covers the alignment of the chord and heavy chain-link fencing precludes much photography. Between Old Trafford and Deansgate Junction the former MSJ&A line now sees only one form of traffic-the Metrolink trams that ply between the Cheshire market town, Manchester centre and Bury-the Lancashire market town famous for black puddings and Sir Robert Peel. Passing the road down to the Bridgewater Canal, LRV No.**1024** pulls nippily away from Timperley and heads towards Navigation Road. *E.M.Johnson*

Soss Moss Lane Overbridge, between Chelford and Alderley Edge, Cheshire, March 27th.1959: The profusion of overhead line equipment for the impending Manchester-Crewe electrification makes this stretch of railway through the beautiful Cheshire countryside look rather untidy. However, modernisation will soon be a fact of railway life along the line here and sights such as "Patriot" 4-6-0 No.**45543** *Home Guard* at the head of the 9.05 am Birmingham New Street to Manchester London Road Express will shortly be history. The sidings in the background served the ROF building at nearby Chelford. *Michael Mensing*

Soss Moss Lane Overbridge, August 10th.1994: The bright, galvanised steelwork of the overhead catenary supports has now blended into the surrounding countryside and electric traction has been a fact of life here for almost 34 years. A Class 90 electric loco rushes past at the head of the 12.00 Euston-Manchester Express. The semaphore signals have gone and cows now stroll contentedly over the land once straddled by the ROF sidings. *E.M.Johnson*

There is little doubt that many enthusiasts have tended to glamourise railway operation over the years. Much of this attention has centred around the steam locomotive with a lot of emotive talk-some of it, frankly, little more than twaddle. It must not be forgotten that, though of primary importance, there was much more to railway operation than just locomotives. In my experience of dealing with and talking to railwaymen over the years, a strong sense of camaraderie comes over and one sensed that, for most of the operating staff, running a railway was a team exercise and each man respected the part that the other played. Drivers and firemen were in charge of locomotives and guards were in charge of trains; but, over all was the "bobby"-the signalman who controlled his section and dictated, via his instruments, levers and signals when and where trains could go. So, by way of a change, we look back to the "good old days"-to 1932 and 1933. John William Smith, of 2, Thurloe Street, Rusholme, Manchester was one of three signalmen employed in the signalbox at Wilbraham Road, on the Chorlton Junction to Fairfield line, in that period. The basic working week for signalmen on the LNER in 1932 was 48 hours. Corresponding pay for this class of box was £2.13.3d. (£2.81) per week. From John Smith's wage card we can learn much about pay and conditions at this time: some enhanced rates seem to have been paid - a rise of 4/ 3d every third week: probably for night duty. Wages just in excess of £4, occuring on six occasions in this period, must have seemed like largesse indeed. In January 1933 Mr.Smith fell ill for three days: seemingly, the LNER allowed no sick pay and poor John received just £1.6.10d. for the week of January 14th. At the end of the month he was unable to work for a complete week and got no pay at all! Further illness developed and another poorly paid week ensued. Were these really "the good old days"? *Author's collection*

Wilbraham Road, Friday, February 4th.1927: John ("Jack") Smith surveys the scene from his little box. Here is a canvas painted with all the detail and order inherent from the days of the pre-Group companies. The neat pallislade fence behind the platform, the little rockery garden at the end of the platform ramp, the artistically-styled Home signal, notice the arched border between the black and white painting below the balance weight. The signalbox itself is built to a typical MS&L standard design; though dimunitive in appearance, these little structures were massively built-solid, reliable artefacts which had been made to last. *G.H.Platt*

Wilbraham Road, c.1946/7: B17 No.**1664** *Liverpool* storms up the 1-in-340 from Chorlton Junction towards Fallowfield with an Up express. *Liverpool* was one of eleven of a third batch of B17 4-6-0s built by Robert Stephenson & Co. in 1937. As built, all were named after football clubs. As 2864 the engine was turned out to traffic on January 15th.1937, acquiring the number 1664 on June 29th.1946. Later becoming 61664, *Liverpool* was condemned on June 1st.1960 and was cut up at Stratford. These engines, conceived originally for traffic on the Great Eastern section of the LNER, would have been a familiar sight to John Smith and to Alban Daly who is pictured at the signalbox window. B17s were used frequently on cross-country trains from Liverpool and Manchester Central to the East Coast ports of Hull and Harwich; superceding GNR Atlantics and GCR "Sir Sam Fay" 4-6-0s on these duties.

William Lees

Woodley Junction c.1866: "The poetry of history," wrote the historian G.M.Trevelyan, "lies in the quasi-miraculous fact that once, on this earth, on this familiar spot of earth, walked other men and women as actual as we are today, thinking their own thoughts, swayed by their own passions but now all gone, vanishing one after another, gone as utterly as we ourselves shall be gone like ghosts at cock-crow."
A picture taken at Woodley Junction, probably upon the inauguration of double track working on the Hyde Junction to New Mills line sometime in 1866. Elsewhere in this book I have spoken of the totally different world portrayed in Victorian and Edwardian scenes. Yet, here at Woodley is something completely beyond even that. This amazing picture, probably one of the oldest railway views taken in this area, shows a passenger train, with locomotives-Sacré outside-framed 0-6-0s-at each end-undergoing what appears to be some sort of inspection. It is likely that the top-hatted official-looking gentlemen could well be Board of Trade officials present prior to the introduction of the new line nearest to the camera. The train is standing on the Down line, the original single line from Hyde Junction to New Mills. Some of the characters could well have come straight off a Wild West set! adorned with Pillbox and Billy-Cock hats and neckerchiefs. In the background is a wooden footbridge later replaced. Beyond this can be seen the bottom flange of the original Hyde Road bridge. This was removed to become a pipe bridge upon the opening of the re-aligned road. Notice the ash-ballasted trackwork covering the sleepers: a common sight in early railway views.
G.K.Fox Collection

Woodley, July 25th.1994: Trevelyan's people have indeed gone like ghosts at cock crow as we look upon Woodley station from the same spot some 128 years later. The little clutch of passengers were awaiting the arrival of the 09.34 all stations Rose Hill to Manchester Piccadilly when I photographed them on a sultry summer morning. Now unstaffed and unloved, Woodley has seen better days: its windows boarded over, its tracks-long bereft of important through passenger and teeming freight services-are now weed-strewn and quiet. The junction where once Midland trains with glorious crimson lake coaches and pretty and majestic green and, later, red engines at their head, rattled past and headed towards Manchester via Hyde Junction is but a very distant memory. Alongside the smart housing estate, built on the site of the former goods yard, a single lead junction spawns two separate running lines: one feeds the Greater Manchester waste disposal plant at Bredbury, the other the Tilcon stone depot on the west side of the former Great Central and Midland Joint line from Romiley to Ashburys. Woodley's heyday has gone.
E.M.Johnson